WHAT FLAG?

WHAT FLAG?

NICOLE SMITH

CHARTWELL
BOOKS

This edition published in 2015 by
CHARTWELL BOOKS
an imprint of Book Sales
a division of Quarto Publishing Group
USA Inc.
142 West 36th Street, 4th Floor
New York, NY 10018
USA

Copyright © 2015
Regency House Publishing Limited
The Manor House
High Street
Buntingford
Hertfordshire
SG9 9AB
United Kingdom

For all editorial enquiries, please contact:
www.regencyhousepublishing.com

ISBN-13: 978-0-7858-3323-9

Printed in China

All photography, maps and flag artwork
© www.shutterstock.com.
Except for pages 111 & 116
© Paul Manley
World map: pages 6–7 courtesy of The
United Nations.

The author and publishers have made every
effort to ensure that the information
contained in this book is accurate at the time
of going to press. They cannot, however,
accept any legal responsibility for omissions
and errors in this publication.

Contents

INTRODUCTION

The foremost property of flags is that each one immediately identifies a particular nation, dependency or territory, without the need for explanation. The colors, shapes, sizes and devices of each flag are often linked to the political evolution of a country, embodying heraldic codes, and often reflect strongly held ideals, past and present philosophies and aspirations.

Flags arouse feelings of patriotism and national pride, and major insult may be caused if such a potent symbol is defiled.

United Nations flag.

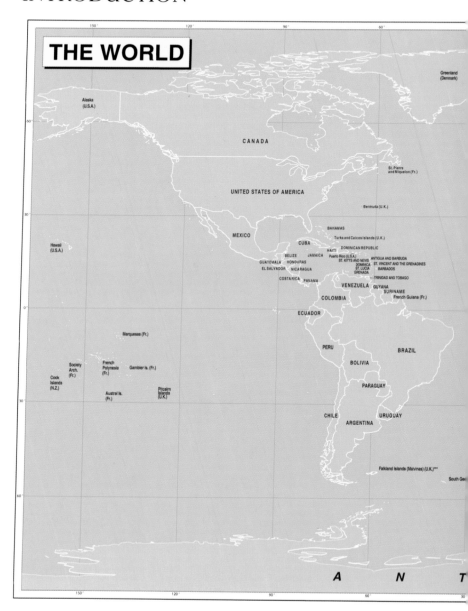

WHAT FLAG?

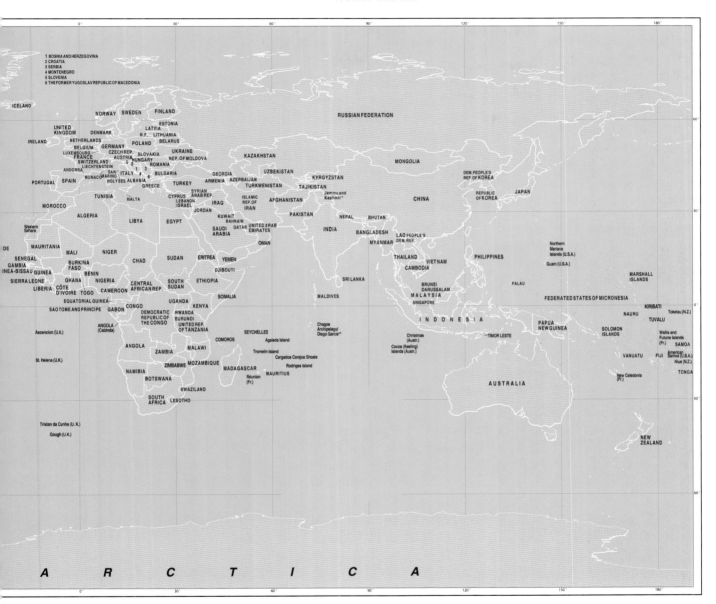

1 BOSNIA AND HERZEGOVINA
2 CROATIA
3 SERBIA
4 MONTENEGRO
5 SLOVENIA
6 THE FORMER YUGOSLAV REPUBLIC OF MACEDONIA

INTRODUCTION

We have become accustomed to the image of a new country marking independence by means of a flag-hoisting ceremony. Very often, the new color or arrangement will intend to signify goodwill, peace or democracy. In recent times, political upheavals in the former Yugoslavia, the former U.S.S.R, East Africa and other nations has led to a revision of boundaries, national identity and

Flag of the International Red Cross.

International maritime signal flags.

often the emergence of new nation states and hence new flags.

The Flag Institute has identified a number of areas of flag activity, all of which are continuing to grow. National flags may be used by governments or flown by private citizens. Flags may be designed for civil and military use. Other flags include those of semi-state institutions (such as national airlines), national institutions (such as the Royal National Lifeboat Institute), political organizations, commercial companies and corporations (with house flags and promotional flags of all kinds) and flags created for individuals. These areas of flag activity are all continuing to grow.

United Nations Office at Geneva, Switzerland.

INTRODUCTION

Commonwealth flag.

European Union flag.

Flags are becoming increasingly important to all organizations throughout the world as powerful and evocative symbols of corporate as well as national identities.

This book is intended for the lay reader who will find it a valuable introduction to the fascination of vexillology (the study of flags). Each continent is dealt with separately to give the reader an appreciation of the overall geography of the region as well as the characteristics of each nation's flag. By examining dependencies, territories, provinces and international organizations, the reader gains a valuable insight into the evolutions of the political world we live in today.

Details of population, capital cities, language and currencies provide a demographic and financial perspective, though these aspects are forever changing, and in some newly emerging countries it would be difficult to predict alterations in currencies or official languages. The information given here is based on the up-to-date facts and figures currently available.

United States of America, state flags.

World flags.

CHAPTER ONE

NORTH AMERICA

WHAT FLAG?

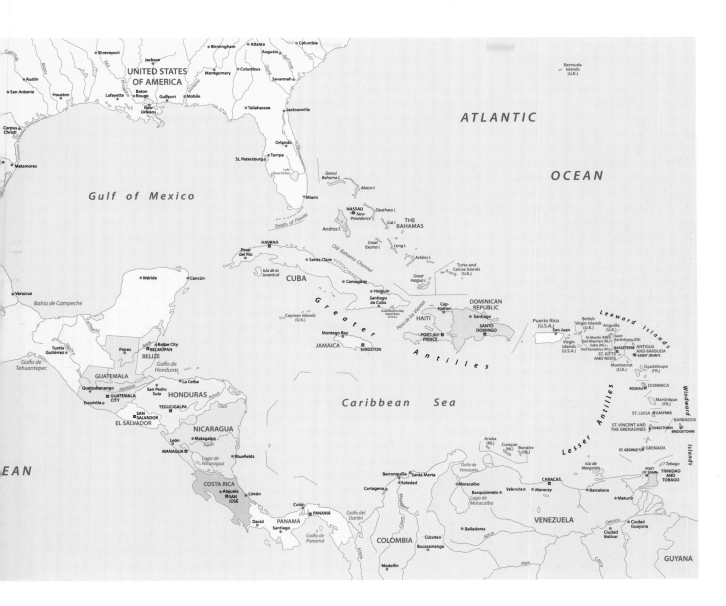

Antigua & Barbuda

Antigua and Barbuda are part of the Leeward Islands. The islands are dependent on tourism, cotton, sugar cane crops and lobster fishing. The flag was introduced as a result of a competition in 1967, when the islands became self-governing. The red background stands for the dynamism of the people, the inverted triangle forming a victory V. The white and the blue stand for the sands and the seas. The yellow rising sun reflects the dawning of a new era and the sky reflects the African heritage. The flag remained unchanged when the country achieved independence in 1981.

Population:	86,295
Capital:	St. John's
Languages:	English
Currency:	East Caribbean dollar

Antigua Bay from Shirely Heights.

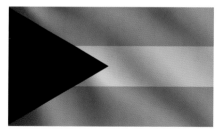

Bahamas

The Bahamas are composed of a coral-limestone archipelago of 700 islands and over 1,000 cays in the western Atlantic. The country's economy is largely dependent on tourism and the islands are characterized by golden beaches and aquamarine waters, the aquamarine and yellow stripes on the flag representing these two features. The black triangle represents the unity of the nation and its inhabitants. This flag was introduced in 1973 when the country became independent.

Population:	368,390
Capital:	Nassau
Languages:	English
Currency:	Bahamian dollar of 100 cents

Tip of Paradise with Nassau in the background, Bahamas.

Barbados

This densely populated island in the West Indies is made up of limestone and coral. The principal source of income of the island is tourism. It was a British colony from 1627 to 1966. The blue and yellow stripes represent the sea, the sky and the golden sands. Neptune's trident relates to the island's dependency on the sea. The shaft of the trident was removed to signify a break with the past and old traditions. The black stands for the African heritage. The flag was adopted in 1966 and was the result of a winning entry in a competition.

Population:	285,000
Capital:	Bridgetown
Languages:	English
Currency:	Barbados dollar

Belize

Belize is an enclave situated on the coast of Central America. Formerly known as British Honduras, Belize gained its independence in 1981, having had a long struggle since 1950. This date is symbolized by the 50 laurel leaves surrounding the center picture. For many years, Belize's main industry was logging, which is reflected in the center of the flag which shows two timber workers with their tools. Beneath the shield is an inscription from the legend *Sub umbra floreo* (I flourish in the shadows). The thin red strips at the top and bottom of the flag symbolize the United Democratic Party.

Population:	358,899
Capital:	Belmopan
Languages:	English
Currency:	Belize dollar

View of Bridgetown, Barbados.

Canada

Canada is the world's second largest country, divided into 10 provinces and two territories, with some 80 per cent of the land uninhabited. The country was still technically under the British Imperial Parliament until 1931, when the creation of the British Commonwealth made the country a sovereign nation under the Crown. Prior to 1965, the British Red Ensign with the Canadian Arms was used, but was unpopular with Canada's French population. The new flag we know today managed to break all affinities with both France and the U.K. and helped to unite the French and British with the indigenous population. The two red stripes either side represent the Pacific and Atlantic Oceans. These were originally meant to be blue but were changed to red, being an official color of Canada. The red also represents the blood shed by Canadians who died in the First World War. The white represents the vast snowy areas in the north of the country, while the maple leaf is the traditional emblem of Canada.

Population:	35,702,707
Capital:	Ottawa
Languages:	French, English
Currency:	Canadian dollar

Toronto, Ontario.

16

Vancouver, British Columbia.

Provinces & Territories of Canada

New Brunswick

Northwest Territories

Alberta

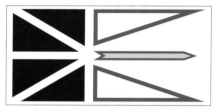

Newfoundland

Nova Scotia

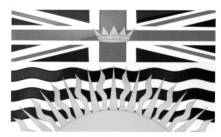

British Columbia

Manitoba

Parliament Hill, Ottawa, Ontario.

WHAT FLAG?

Ontario

Saskatchewan

Yukon Territory

Prince Edward Island

Québec

Moraine Lake, Banff National Park, British Columbia.

Costa Rica

Costa Rica lies in Central America with the Pacific Ocean on one side and the Atlantic on the other. Mountain ranges run through the whole length of the country. In 1824, Costa Rica gained independence and became a member of the Central American Federation along with Guatemala, Honduras and Nicaragua. This flag derives from the CAF flag, but has been altered to include a red stripe through the center.

Population:	4,733,130
Capital:	San José
Languages:	Spanish
Currency:	Colón of 100 centavos

A view of the Arenal Volcano from the tropical forest, Costa Rica.

Cuba

Cuba is the largest island in the Caribbean. It has a varied landscape ranging from mountainous areas to fertile plains. Originally discovered by Christopher Colombus in 1492, the Spanish began to arrive from 1511. Cuba finally achieved independence in 1898 and developed a strong relationship with the U.S.A. In 1959, the right-wing dictator Fulgencio Batista was overthrown by Marxist revolutionary forces led by Fidel Castro. Cuba's new ally became the U.S.S.R. This flag was designed in 1849, but was not in use until 1901 when the Spanish finally withdrew from the island. The red triangle represents the blood shed during the struggle for independence.

Population:	11,210,064
Capital:	Havana
Languages:	Spanish
Currency:	Peso of 100 centavos

Havana, Cuba.

Dominica

Dominica is a mountainous island situated in the Caribbean and largely dependent on tourism. Dominica gained independence from Britain in 1978 after 11 years as a self-governing U.K. colony. The parrot on the flag is a sisserou, the national bird, only found on the island, and taken from a coat of arms. The stars represent the 10 island parishes, the red disc socialism, the green background the country's vegetation and the cross Christianity, the three colors of the cross representing the Holy Trinity. The black stripe symbolizes the people's African origins, the yellow the Carib people and, as ever, the white is for peace and purity.

Altos de Chavón, Dominican Republic.

Dominica.

Population:	71,293
Capital:	Roseau
Languages:	English
Currency:	East Caribbean dollar

Dominican Republic

Situated in the Caribbean, the Dominican Republic shares the island of Hispaniola, with Haiti occupying the western third. Once a Spanish colony, the country gained independence in 1821. Haiti then held the territory until 1844, when sovereignty was restored, the flag having evolved during this period of Haitian rule. The flag's design stems from the Haitian flag but a white cross was added and the colors in the corners were rearranged.

Population: 10,378,267
Capital: Santo Domingo
Languages: Spanish
Currency: Peso of 100 centavos

Pre-Columbian ruins, San Andrés, El Salvador.

El Salvador

El Salvador is a small Central American country lying along the Pacific Ocean. Behind the coastal plain, where the majority of the population lives, are high rugged mountains and volcanoes. Civil war broke out in 1979 which wrecked the country, leaving the economy in tatters and many people homeless. However, a cease-fire took effect in 1992, but the country remains in a poor state. El Salvador gained independence from Spain in 1821, although the current flag dates only to 1912. (Blue and white flags are common in Central American countries which gained independence from Spain.)

Population: 6,401,240
Capital: San Salvador
Languages: Spanish
Currency: El Salvador colón

Grenada

Situated in the Windward Islands, Grenada, nicknamed the Isle of Spice, also includes the Southern Grenadines. Grenada was a British colony from 1783 to 1974 when it became completely independent. Following a coup in 1979, the government was controlled by the Marxist Maurice Bishop. In 1983, Bishop was executed in a further coup and to put an end to the ensuing chaos, the U.S. sent in troops to restore democracy. Dating from independence in 1974, the seven stars on the flag symbolize Grenada's seven parishes. A major export is nutmeg, which is depicted within the triangle to the left of centre. Red stands for unity among the people, yellow for friendliness and sunshine, while green is for the island.

Population: 103,328
Capital: St. George's
Languages: English
Currency: East Caribbean dollar

Guatemala

Guatemala is a highly populated country, sharing a mountainous terrain with both the Pacific and Caribbean coastlines. The country was first conquered by the Spanish in the 1520s, remaining under Spanish control until 1821 when independence was finally granted. The flag was adopted in 1871, but its origins date back to the Central American Federation (1823–1839), which was set up following the break from Spain in 1821. The CAF included Costa Rica, El Salvador, Honduras, Nicaragua and Guatemala. The blue and white stripes are common to many Central and South American countries. About half its people still speak the ancient Mayan language.

Population:	15,806,675
Capital:	Guatemala City
Languages:	Spanish, Mayan
Currency:	Quetzal

Haiti

Haiti, a mountainous country, is the second largest island nation in the Caribbean and takes up a third of Hispaniola. It was a French colony from 1697 to 1804 and remains French-speaking. The country has been dogged by instability, coups and corruption. Multi-party elections were introduced in the 1990s, but in 1991 the military took over in the wake of the deposition of President Jean-Bertrand Aristide, who was restored to office in 1994 with the help of U.S. troops. The flag adopted around the time of independence derives from the French tricolor, although it has now developed into a horizontal arrangement of colors. The red band represents the mulatto community

View of Antigua from Cerro de la Cruz, Guatemala.

and the blue the black community. The official flag shows the country's arms on a white background with the motto 'Unity is strength' in the center and a palm tree surrounded by weapons.

Population: 10,911,819
Capital: Port-au-Prince
Languages: French
Currency: Gourde

Honduras

Like many others in Central America, Honduras is a mountainous country.

Mayan ruins in Copán, Honduras.

The Spanish conquered the country in the 1520s and plundered it for precious metals. It achieved independence in 1838. Mining remained important and is still an integral part of the economy. Honduras was one of the five members of the Central American Federation consisting of Honduras, Guatemala, El Salvador, Nicaragua and Costa Rica, the flag, officially adopted in 1949, having derived from the CAF arrangements of the other members. The five stars symbolize the hope that the five nations may eventually become a federation of states.

Population: 8,725,111
Capital: Tegucigalpa
Languages: Spanish
Currency: Lempira

Haitian beach.

Jamaica

Jamaica is one of the largest of the Caribbean islands, with much of the terrain being upland with tropical vegetation and high rainfall. The hated slavery trade was centered in Jamaica until it was dispersed in 1834. Independence from Britain arrived in 1962 when the flag was adopted. The gold color represents the country's mineral wealth and sunshine, the green is for its agriculture and for hope, and the black for the hardships that the people have faced in the past through slavery.

Population:	2,717,911
Capital:	Kingston
Languages:	English
Currency:	Jamaican dollar

Mexico

Mexico is the largest Spanish-speaking nation in the world and has a wide variety of physical features ranging from large areas of open basin-and-range to mountains and active volcanoes. The country became independent in 1821 and it was at this time that the green, white and red stripes were established, although the current flag was adopted in 1823. Mexico's arms, in the center of the flag, are based on an Aztec legend and feature an eagle devouring a snake while perched on top of a cactus on an island in a lake. This is the Aztec symbol for Mexico City.

Population:	121,005,815
Capital:	Mexico City
Languages:	Spanish
Currency:	Peso

Colonial church, Jamaica.

Chichén Itzá, Mexico.

Nicaragua

Nicaragua is one of the larger countries in Central America. It has a varied landscape, its mountain ranges bisected by fertile valleys and a large coastal plain. Until 1821, Nicaragua was part of the captaincy-general of Guatemala, which was ruled by Spain. In that year, Nicaragua declared independence, but this was short-lived as Nicaragua quickly became part of the Mexican Empire, breaking away in 1823. It then became part of the United Provinces of Central America, but left this union in 1838. The Nicaraguan flag, dating from 1908, is very similar to that of El Salvador, except for the shade of blue and the motif in center.

Population:	6,134,270
Capital:	Managua
Languages:	Spanish
Currency:	Córdoba

Cathedral of Leon Nicaragua.

Panama

With a hot, humid climate, Panama is a tiny country linking North and South America. Panama also links the Pacific and Atlantic Oceans with its canal. In 1903, Panama achieved its independence from Colombia, of which it had once been a province. Since independence, Panama's government has changed many times. The flag dates back to 1903. Inspired by the Stars and Stripes, the blue stands for the Conservative Party, white for hope and peace and red for the Liberal Party. The red star stands for law and order and the blue star for civic virtues.

Population:	3,764,166
Capital:	Panama City
Languages:	Spanish
Currency:	Balboa, U.S. dollar

The Panama Canal.

St. Christopher & Nevis

Situated in the Lesser Antilles, St. Christopher (also known as St. Kitts) and Nevis consists of two islands. Originally colonized by Britain in 1713, the islands became independent in 1983 when this flag was adopted, having been designed by a student as an entry in a competition. The colors represent green for fertility, yellow for sunshine, red for the struggle for independence, and black for the people's African heritage. The two stars symbolize hope and freedom. The colors of the flag are also associated with Rastafarianism.

Population:	55,000
Capital:	Basseterre
Languages:	English
Currency:	East Caribbean dollar

St. Christopher.

St. Lucia

Situated in the Caribbean, St. Lucia was first settled by France in 1650 but became British in 1814. It then changed hands, alternating between the two countries many times. St. Lucia gained full independence from Britain in 1979, the flag dating back to 1967 when the country became internally self-governing and an Associated State of Great Britain. The symbol in the center of the flag represents the Pitons, twin conical volcanic plugs that rise impressively from the sea, with the yellow representing golden sands and sun.

Population:	185,000
Capital:	Castries
Languages:	English
Currency:	East Caribbean dollar

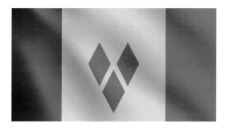

St. Vincent & the Grenadines

St. Vincent and the Grenadines are islands in the Lesser Antilles. The country became a British colony in 1783, self-governing in 1969 and finally independent in 1979. The flag

The Pitons, St. Lucia.

Lower Bay, St. Vincent & the Grenadines.

is based on a design first used on independence and was the result of a winning entry in a competition. The three green diamonds, representing the islands as the 'gems of the Antilles', were added in 1985 and replaced the island's coat of arms.

Population:	109,000
Capital:	Kingstown
Languages:	English
Currency:	East Caribbean dollar

Trinidad & Tobago

Trinidad and Tobago are two islands lying off the coast of Venezuela, which have been linked politically since the late 19th century. First discovered by Christopher Columbus in 1498, the islands were settled by the French and Spanish and then by the British. The state became independent in 1962 when the flag was adopted, with red for the warmth of the sun and for the determination and courage of the people, black for their strength and white for the surf of the sea.

Population:	1,328,019
Capital:	Port-of-Spain
Languages:	English
Currency:	Trinidad & Tobago dollar

Englishman's Bay, Tobago.

31

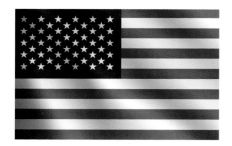

United States of America

The United States of America is a federation of 50 states and is the world's fourth largest country. The U.S.A., being so large, has an enormous variety of landscapes and climates. In 1776, it declared independence from Britain and set up a federal republic, the flag having first been adopted in 1777 during the War of Independence. The flag is known as the 'Stars and Stripes' and has become one of the most recognizable in the world, with the stars on the blue canton representing the 50 states and the 13 red and white stripes the 13 original colonies which declared independence from the British.

Population: 320,892,000
Capital: Washington, D.C.
Languages: English
Currency: U.S. dollar

The Capitol, Washington, D.C.

Stoneman Bridge, Yosemite National Park.

United States of America

Arkansas

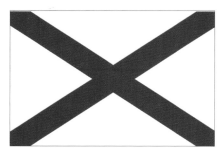

Alabama

Alaska

Arizona

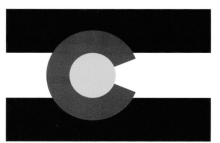

Colorado

California

Connecticut

Humpback whales frolicking in the ocean, Juneau, Alaska.

DECEMBER 7, 1787

Delaware

City skyline and Bridge of Lions, St. Augustine, Florida.

Florida

Georgia

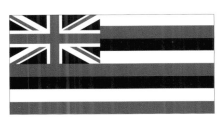

Hawaii

Idaho

Illinois

Kansas

Louisiana

Indiana

Chicago skyline with the Hancock Tower in the centre.

Iowa

Kentucky

Maine

Maryland

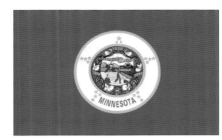

Minnesota

Mississippi

Massachusetts

Michigan

Big Sable Point Lighthouse, Mason County, Michigan.

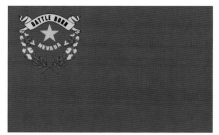

Nevada

New Hampshire

Missouri

Montana

Nebraska

Valley of Fire State Park near Las Vegas, Nevada.

WHAT FLAG?

New York

New Jersey

New Mexico

Manhattan midtown skyline and the Hudson river, New York.

North Carolina

North Dakota

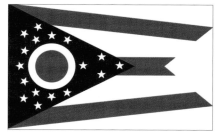

Ohio

Great Smoky Mountains National Park, North Carolina.

Oklahoma

Oregon

Pennsylvania

Philadelphia, Pennsylvania.

Rhode Island

Tennessee

Texas

South Carolina

South Dakota

Mount Rushmore, South Dakota.

WHAT FLAG?

Utah

Vermont

Virginia

Salt Lake City, Utah.

CHAPTER TWO

SOUTH AMERICA

Argentina

Known as the 'Land of Silver', Argentina is the world's eighth largest country, having emerged as a nation state in 1816. With the Andes mountains to the west, much of central Argentina is covered by pampas grasslands, with Patagonia covering

Congress building, Buenos Aires, Argentina.

La Paz, Bolivia.

the region to the far south. Argentina lays claim to the South Atlantic islands and part of Antarctica, and unsuccessfully invaded the Falkland Islands (Islas Malvinas) in 1982. The blue and white triband was adopted by demonstrators following independence from the Spanish in 1810. The Sun of May was also adopted about the same time and represents the sun that shone through the clouds on 25 May 1810 when the demonstrations first began in Buenos

Aires. The flag was first hoisted by General Manuel Belgrano in 1812 when he was leading the revolution.

Population:	43,131,966
Capital:	Buenos Aires
Languages:	Spanish
Currency:	Argentine peso

Bolivia

Bolivia, formerly Upper Peru, is today one of the poorest South American republics. It is a landlocked country which includes an area of the Andes and to the south-west covers part of the Amazon basin. Bolivia boasts Lake Titicaca, the highest navigable body of water in the world. Independence was established from the Spanish in 1825, who exploited its silver reserves. Bolivia was named at this time after its first president, El Liberador (The Liberator), Simon Bolívar. The flag has been the national emblem since 1888.

WHAT FLAG?

The red stands for Bolivia's animals and the army's courage, the yellow for the metal resources and the green for the agricultural richness of the country.

Population: 11,410,651
Capital: La Paz

Languages: Spanish, Quechua, Aymara
Currency: Boliviano

Flamingos, Lake Hedionda, Bolivia.

Brazil

Brazil is a huge country covering nearly half of South America and is the fifth largest in the world. It is a federation of 23 states and four

territories, including the Federal District. Brazil is home to the world's largest rain forest which is undergoing a rapid process of deforestation. Brazil declared itself independent from Portugal in 1822. In 1889, it became a republic, but there were years of dictatorships and military rule before democracy returned in 1990. The sphere on the flag bears the motto *Ordem e progresso*, which means 'Order and progress', the Brazilian states represented by the stars. The arrangement of stars is the night sky over Rio de Janeiro on the day the emperor abdicated on 15 November 1889. Green represents the rain forests and the yellow diamond the country's mineral wealth.

Population:	204,234,000	**Languages:**	Portuguese
Capital:	Brasilia	**Currency:**	Real

View of Christ the Redeemer and Corcovado Mountain, Rio de Janeiro, Brazil.

The Devil's Throat, Iguazu Falls, Brazil.

Chile

Chile occupies the south-west coast of South America, together with several South Pacific islands. It is the thinnest of the world's large countries, forming a narrow strip along the western coast of the continent. Chile was a Spanish colony from the 16th century, but became independent on 1 January 1818. The design of the flag stems from this period and it is said to have been designed by an American called Charles Wood, in the service of the freedom fighters. There is little doubt that the inspiration for this flag stems from the Stars and Stripes, with white representing the snow-capped Andes, blue the sky and red the blood of those who sacrificed their lives for freedom.

Population:	18,006,407
Capital:	Santiago
Languages:	Spanish
Currency:	Chilean peso

Colombia

Christopher Columbus discovered what was to become known as Colombia in 1499, the Spanish conquest beginning some years later. Colombia emerged as an independent state from the Spanish Vice-Royalty of New Granada in 1819, and the flag was adopted at this time. Colombia

Bogotá and the Santamaria Bullring, Columbia.

Torres del Paine National Park, Chile.

has suffered from instability with two civil wars. Its economy is based largely on crops, including coffee, bananas and cotton, although it has been said that the main contribution to the Colombian economy comes from drugs. The yellow represents the nation of Colombia, the blue the sea and the severance of the domination by the Spanish. Finally, the red represents the loss of blood of the people during the fighting.

Population: 48,103,900
Capital: Bogotá
Languages: Spanish
Currency: Colombian peso

Ecuador

Straddling the equator, it is from this geographical location that Ecuador took its name. Ecuador has a variety of landscapes, with high mountainous regions, an eastern alluvial area and a coastal plain. Its flag is shared in different adaptations by Colombia and Venezuela, the colors having been adopted by freedom fighter Francisco de Miranda in 1806. Independence was finally achieved from Spain in 1822, when Ecuador became part of Gran Colombia, with full independence coming in 1830.

The Cotopaxi volcano looms over a church in the Valle de los Chillos, Ecuador.

Population: 15,466,000
Capital: Quito
Languages: Spanish
Currency: U.S. dollar

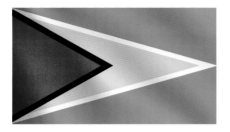

Jesuit mission ruins in Trinidad, Paraguay.

Guyana

Guyana means 'land of many waters' and faces the Atlantic Ocean in north-eastern South America. The coastal area is below sea level with dykes to prevent flooding. Formerly known as British Guiana, Guyana gained independence from the U.K. in 1966 and adopted this flag. The red triangle represents the people's energy in building a new nation, the black border being for endurance and perseverance. The red arrowhead symbolizes the country's mineral resources, while the white is for the rivers and green for the land.

Population:	746,900
Capital:	Georgetown
Languages:	English
Currency:	Guyanese dollar

Paraguay

Paraguay is a landlocked country in South America. With a history of internal strife and conflict with its neighbors, Paraguay has had many setbacks, and was one of the first South American countries to gain independence from the Spanish in

Kaieteur Falls, Guyana.

1811. At this time, the tricolor flag was adopted, although it was not until a year later, in 1812, that the red, white, and blue color scheme was established. The coat of arms was added in 1821 and depicts the Star of May in honour of independence on 14 May. On the reverse side of the flag is the treasury seal consisting of a lion and staff, with the words 'Peace and Justice'. This was added in 1842.

Population:	7,003,406
Capital:	Asunción
Languages:	Spanish, Guaraní
Currency:	Guaraní

The triple frontiers of Brazil, Paraguay and Argentina on the Parana and Iguazu rivers.

Machu Picchu, a 15th-century Inca site, Peru.

Languages: Spanish, Quechua
Currency: Nuevo sol

Peru

Lying in western South America, Peru is made up of a narrow coastal plain, the mountain range of the Andes with part of the Amazon basin in the east. The Amerindians first arrived in Peru about 12,000 years ago. In the 16th century the country was conquered by the Spanish, with Peru finally gaining

Lima Cathedral, Peru.

The Cathedral-Basilica of Sts. Peter and Paul, Paramaribo, Suriname.

independence from Spain in 1824 but, since then, development has been slow with an unbalanced economy. Peru's flag dates from 1825, the white representing peace and justice and red the people who lost their lives in the struggle for independence. The color scheme dates from 1820 when the great liberation leader General José de San Martin claimed that a flock of red and white flamingos flew over his marching troops.

Population: 31,151,643
Capital: Lima

Suriname

Suriname, formerly Dutch Guiana, lies between French Guiana and Guyana in the north-east of South America. The British were the first Europeans to colonize the country, but soon after, in 1667, the British handed over the territory to the Dutch. Suriname is a land of mixed races and religions, with people of African, Asian and European descent making up the bulk of the population. Independence arrived in 1975 although the country still relies heavily on the Dutch for aid. The flag, adopted in 1975, features the colors of the main political parties, the star standing for the unity of all the peoples and for altruism.

Population: 534,189
Capital: Paramaribo
Languages: Dutch
Currency: Suriname dollar

Uruguay

Uruguay is officially known as the Eastern Republic of Uruguay, and is South America's second smallest independent state. It was the last Latin-American territory to secure its independence, in this case from Brazil, which came in 1828. Uruguay's flag dates from 1830, the nine blue and white stripes symbolizing the nine provinces of Uruguay when it became independent. The colors of the flag and the Sun of May were taken from the Argentinian flag which represented the struggle against Spanish rule.

Population:	3,404,189
Capital:	Montevideo
Languages:	Spanish
Currency:	Uruguayan peso

Venezuela

Venezuela (Little Venice) is situated in the north of South America. It was first discovered by Christopher Columbus in 1498 and later became part of the Spanish territory of New Granada. The country has a common history with Colombia and Ecuador and the three countries share similar flags, the yellow, blue and red being the colors of the Venezuelan freedom fighter, Francisco de Miranda. Blue is for the sea which divides Venezuela and its other dominions from Spain, which is represented by red and yellow. The seven stars represent the seven provinces of the Venezuelan Federation.

Population:	30,620,404
Capital:	Caracas
Languages:	Spanish
Currency:	Bolívar

Lighthouse in José Ignacio, near Punta del Este, Uruguay.

Caracas, Venezuela.

CHAPTER THREE

EUROPE

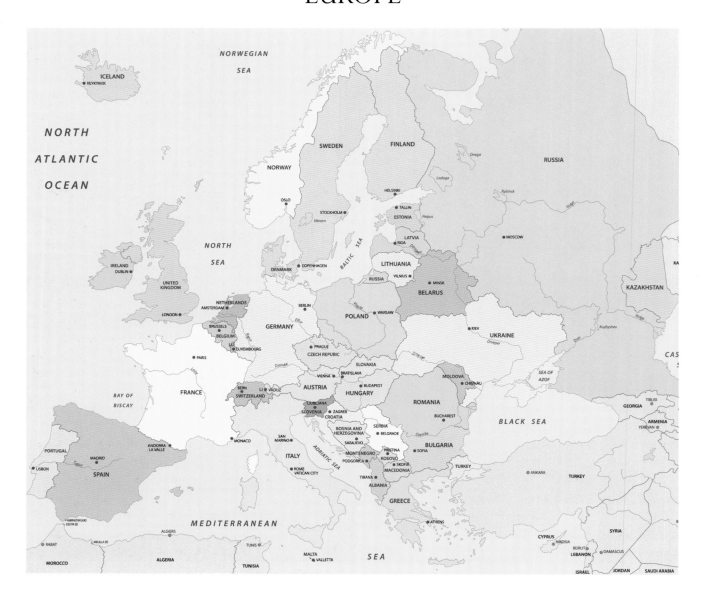

El Tarter ski resort, Andorra.

Albania

Albania is a small country with a mountainous interior bordering the Adriatic Sea. It was ruled by the Communists from 1944 until a non-communist government took over in 1992, but the years of isolation have left Albania the poorest country in Europe. Since 1912, Albania has used a flag with a double-headed black eagle, this having been adopted by the national hero Iskander Bey (Skanderbeg) when Albania was part of the Ottoman Empire. Skanderbeg drove the Turks from Albania in 1443. The red background to this flag symbolizes the blood shed in the nation's various struggles for independence.

Population:	2,893,005
Capital:	Tirana (Tiranë)
Languages:	Albanian
Currency:	Lek

Andorra

A tiny, remote country located high in the Pyrenees, Andorra's economy is mainly dependent on tourism and duty-free sales. Dating from 1866, the colors in the flag are said to reflect the principality's joint Franco-Spanish suzerainty, combining the red and blue of the French flag and the yellow of the Spanish. The flag also carries a coat of arms superimposed on the central yellow stripe; this bears the motto 'United strength is greater', reflecting the Franco-Spanish link. The mitre and crozier represent the Bishop of Urgel, the three red stripes on yellow, the Compte de Foix, an agreement between the two in 1278 having been responsible for the links with France and Spain. A democratic constitution was adopted in 1994.

Berat Bridge, Albania.

Population:	76,949
Capital:	Andorra la Vella
Languages:	Catalan
Currency:	Euro

Population:	8,579,747	**Languages:**	German
Capital:	Vienna	**Currency:**	Euro

The ruins of Aggstein Castle on the Danube, Austria.

Austria

Austria is predominantly a country of mountains and forests with permanent snow and glaciers on the higher areas. Most of its population lives in the east. Austria is a neutral country, pledged by law and treaties after the Second World War; but it joined the European Union in 1995. It was occupied by the Germans in 1938, and then by the Allies in 1945, and the modern state did not regain full independence until 1955. The flag dates back to 1191 to the Siege of Acre during the Third Crusade, when it is said that the only part of Duke Leopold V's tunic not bloodstained was beneath his swordbelt. The design was officially adopted in 1918 with the dissolution of the Austro-Hungarian Empire, although the colors had been in use since 1230.

Belarus

Belarus or 'White Russia' became independent from the U.S.S.R. on 19 September 1991. The country had been part of the Russian Empire since 1795, but officially became part of the U.S.S.R. in 1921. It is a low-lying, landlocked country, with extensive forested areas. A Communist Republic within the Soviet Union, Belarus was one of the founding members of the Commonwealth of Independent States. The Belarusian flag consists of a wide, red horizontal stripe on top of a narrower green horizontal stripe. The left side of the flag features a vertical white strip with a red-and-white pattern along its border. The green symbolizes the future, and is the color of hope and revival. The red represents Belarus' bloody past and the decorative pattern the country's rich cultural heritage.

Population:	9,481,000
Capital:	Minsk
Languages:	Belarusian, Russian
Currency:	Belarusian ruble

Mir Castle, Belarus.

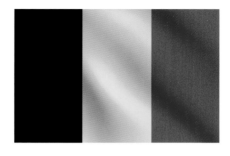

Belgium

United as one of the 'Low Countries' after the Napoleonic Wars, Belgium has quite a varied terrain, with the Ardennes lying to the south-east of the country and comprising moorland, woodland and peat bogs, and the lowland plains making up the rest. The Kingdom of Belgium is strategically placed within Europe, its population consisting of Dutch Flemish-speaking and French Walloon-speaking peoples with a small German minority. Each province has its own flag, that of Belgium deriving from the arms of the provinces of Brabant, Flanders and Hainault. Although the flag is based on the French tricolor, it is interesting to note that it is almost square in shape.

Population:	11,239,755
Capital:	Brussels
Languages:	Dutch, French, German
Currency:	Euro

Mont des Arts, Brussels, Belgium.

Bosnia & Herzegovina

After declaring independence in 1992, Bosnia-Herzegovina was in a state of extreme chaos. It has a population dominated by Muslims with a slightly lesser number of Serbs and a minority of Croats. The Serbs within Bosnia, and from the other side of the border, would not accept the Muslim-Croat alliance and the Muslim-dominated government was perpetually under attack. It wasn't until 1995 that NATO and the UN became involved, which eventually led to an end of the fighting and orderly elections in September 1996. The current flag consists of a blue base with white five-pointed stars crossing the flag diagonally and vertically. Above and below are two half stars. The current flag was adopted in 1998 replacing the previous one which was adopted in 1992. The three points of the triangle stand for the three constituent peoples of Bosnia & Herzegovina: Bosniaks, Croats, and Serbs. The white stars represent Europe and are meant to be infinite in number.

Population:	3,791,622
Capital:	Sarajevo
Languages:	Serbo-Croatian
Currency:	Bosnian convertible marka

Bulgaria

Bulgaria is situated in south-eastern Europe, with its coastline on the Black Sea. Once ruled by the Turks as part of the Ottoman Empire, the country was liberated by Russian forces in 1878. Bulgaria remained heavily dependent on Russia and later, after 1944, on the U.S.S.R. However, the Communist government fell in 1990, since when, Bulgaria has been moving to a market economy. Today's flag was first adopted in 1878, after liberation. White represents peace, green stands for freedom and red for the blood shed by the freedom fighters. There can sometimes be an emblem on the flag which was introduced in 1947, but is now only used on official government occasions.

Population:	7,202,189
Capital:	Sofia
Languages:	Bulgarian
Currency:	Lev

Mostar Bridge, Bosnia & Herzegovina.

Byzantine basilica, Nessebar, Bulgaria.

Croatia

Croatia has a long coastline along the Adriatic Sea. With the outbreak of war in 1991, Croatia suffered some of the worst privations in what was once the former Yugoslavia. The war disrupted the economy, especially the tourist industry, which was a major source of foreign exchange, and manufacturing for the export market was also affected. Croatia's flag dates back to 1848, the arms symbolizing the various regions of the country.

Population:	4,267,558
Capital:	Zagreb
Languages:	Croatian
Currency:	Kuna

Czech Republic

The Czech Republic, formerly part of Czechoslovakia, consists of two areas; Bohemia to the west and Moravia. In 1989 the Communist system was replaced by a multi-party democracy. This was a difficult transition and an upsurge of Slovak nationalism in 1992 resulted in the break-up of Czechoslovakia, although ultimately the split was amicable. The split took place on 1 January 1993, the Czech Republic adopting the flag of the former Czechoslovakia. The red and white represent Bohemia, the blue triangle Moravia and Slovakia.

Population:	10,538,275
Capital:	Prague
Languages:	Czech
Currency:	Koruna

Dubrovnik, Croatia.

The Charles Bridge and the old town, Prague, Czech Republic.

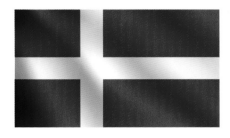

Denmark

The mainland part of Denmark is an extension of the North German Plain, known as the Jutland Peninsula. Denmark also includes 406 islands of which 89 are inhabited. Denmark is one of the oldest monarchies in Europe and at one time had a large empire. The Faroe Islands and

Greenland are still dependencies, but have a large degree of autonomy. The Danish flag is possibly one of the oldest flags in continuous use. It dates back to 1219, when King Waldemar II saw a vision of a white cross in the sky before the Battle of Lyndanisse, the red background representing the sullen evening sky of that night. The flag is known as the Dannebrog (the spirit of Denmark), the off-center cross being common to all the flags of the Scandinavian countries.

Population:	5,659,715
Capital:	Copenhagen
Languages:	Danish
Currency:	Danish krone

Copenhagen, Denmark.

The Little Mermaid, Copenhagen, Denmark.

Estonia

The smallest of the Baltic States, Estonia lies south of the Gulf of Finland with the Baltic Sea to the west. Once part of the Russian Empire, the Baltic States became part of the U.S.S.R. in 1940. Estonia and the other two Baltic States, Latvia and Lithuania, became independent in 1990. The flag was first used in 1918 and continued in use until 1940. It was re-adopted in 1988. The color blue represents the sky, black is for the earth and white for the snows of Estonia's long winter.

Population:	1,312,252
Capital:	Tallinn
Languages:	Estonian
Currency:	Euro

The Viru Gate in the old city of Tallinn, Estonia.

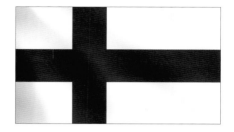

Finland

One of the most northerly states of mainland Europe. Part of Finland lies within the Arctic Circle, and is known as the 'Land of the Midnight Sun', which can be experienced for more days the farther north one travels. At Finland's northernmost point, the sun does not set for 73 consecutive days during summer, and not at all for 51 days during winter. Finland has a history of Russian and Swedish influence, but became independent in 1917 after the collapse of the Russian Empire. It joined the European Union in 1995. The present flag was adopted soon after independence. The colors symbolize Finland's lakes (blue) and snow (white), the off-center cross being typical of Scandinavian flags.

Population: 5,478,002
Capital: Helsinki
Languages: Finnish, Swedish
Currency: Euro

Reindeer in Lapland, Finland.

Helsinki, Finland.

France

After the Ukraine and Russia, France is the third largest country in Europe. It is composed of a wide variety of landscapes, including four upland areas: the Alps, the Pyrenees, the Massifs of Britanny and the Central

Sénanque Abbey, Provence, France.

Plateau. The large lowland areas are drained by rivers such as the Garonne, Rhône, Loire and Seine. France has had a long history: the earliest conquerors were the Romans in 50 B.C. and the latest were the Germans who invaded in both World Wars, although Germany is now one of France's closest allies. The flag dates back to the Revolution of 1789 and is one of the most recognizable in the world. Called the tricolor, it is said to represent Liberty, Equality, Fraternity, signifying the Republican ideal.

Population:	66,121,000
Capital:	Paris
Languages:	French
Currency:	Euro

Paris, France.

Mont-Saint-Michel in Normandy, France.

The ramparts of Carcassonne, France.

Germany

Germany stretches from the North and Baltic Seas in the north to the Alps in the south. The reunification of East and West Germany in 1990 caused many problems, not least the huge cost of reconstruction. Since those challenging times, however, Germany has risen to be a financially strong country and the most successful exporting nation in the European Union. The new Germany not only retained the name, the Federal Republic of Germany, but also kept the original West German flag, the red, black and gold colors dating from the days of the Holy Roman Empire.

Population:	81,083,600
Capital:	Berlin
Languages:	German
Currency:	Euro

The Reichstag, Berlin, Germany.

Neuschwanstein Castle, Bavaria, Germany.

Greece

Greece has a mainland area extending into the Mediterranean Sea and around 2,000 islands, mainly in the Aegean Sea. Greece has been ruled by the Romans and the Turks over the centuries, but finally became independent in the early 19th century.

At one time, the flag was a single blue cross, but this has since given way to the present flag. The cross represents Christianity and blue and white are the national colors of Greece, the blue for the sea and sky and white for the purity of the freedom fighters who established Greece's independence.

Population:	10,992,589
Capital:	Athens
Languages:	Greek
Currency:	Euro

Hungary

Hungary is situated in south-eastern Europe and consists of two lowland plains encompassing some of the most fertile land in Europe. Hungary was defeated in the First World War when much of its territory was divided between Yugoslavia, Romania, and Czechoslovakia. In 1944, Hungary was occupied by the Red Army and a Communist State was established by

Vajdahunyad Castle, Budapest, Hungary.

1949, with Hungary becoming one of the many Eastern European states dominated by the U.S.S.R. An uprising in 1956 against Soviet domination was brutally quashed by Soviet troops, but led the way for more progressive governments and a stronger degree of autonomy from the U.S.S.R. The colors of the Hungarian flag date back to the 15th century, although the flag was first adopted in 1919. The state emblem, first added in 1949, was removed in 1957.

Population:	9,849,000
Capital:	Budapest
Languages:	Magyar
Currency:	Forint

Acropolis and Parthenon, Athens, Greece.

Blarney Castle, Ireland.

Iceland

Far out in the North Atlantic Ocean, Iceland is part of the mid-Atlantic ridge where the two great plates of North America and Europe meet. As a result, Iceland has many volcanoes, geysers and numerous other features relating to volcanic activity. Iceland has a long history of Scandinavian domination, with Norway and Denmark having both been former rulers of the island. In 1944, Iceland became fully independent from Denmark following a referendum in which 97 per cent of the people voted for independence. The flag dates back to 1915 but became official on independence from Denmark. The off-center cross, typical of Scandinavian flags, harks back to a Danish legend and the colors are linked to other Scandinavian countries.

Ireland

The Republic of Ireland occupies 80 per cent of the island of Ireland, the remaining 20 per cent being part of the United Kingdom of Great Britain and Northern Ireland. In 1921, Ireland became an independent state, having been part of the United Kingdom for over 100 years. The flag dates back to 1848 and was used by freedom fighters in their struggle against the British. This came in the wake of the revolutions that were sweeping Europe in 1848 against post-Napoleonic conservatism. The flag was officially adopted after independence, the green representing the Roman Catholic Church, the orange the Protestants, with white symbolizing the desire for peace.

Haifoss Waterfall, Iceland.

Population:	329,100
Capital:	Reykjavik
Languages:	Icelandic
Currency:	Icelandic króna

Population:	4,609,600
Capital:	Dublin
Languages:	Irish, English
Currency:	Euro

Tuscany, Italy.

Italy

Italy is dominated by two mountain ranges: the Alps and the Apennines, which are separated by fertile plains, the islands of Sardinia and Sicily being also part of Italy. The north and south of Italy are very different in terms of culture and wealth, the north being more prosperous than the south. Italy became a united country in 1861 when King Victor Emmanuel was proclaimed ruler. The flag dates back to Napoleonic times and was derived from the French tricolor, but with the blue stripe replaced by a green one, inspired by the shirts of the Milan militia. It has been said, however, that the green was chosen by Napoleon as a personal preference when he invaded Italy in the late 18th century.

Population:	60,788,845
Capital:	Rome
Languages:	Italian
Currency:	Euro

Kosovo

Kosovo is a disputed land-locked territory bordering Serbia, Montenegro, Albania and Macedonia. After a bloody struggle for national self-determination, Kosovo first declared independence from Serbia in February 2008. But it wasn't until July 2010 that the United Nations voted Kosovo's declaration as not having violated international law although, even to this day, Kosovo has yet to obtain full international recognition, with Russia and China still to agree on the legality of Kosovo's existence.

The flag of Kosovo features the geographical shape of the country in gold, centered on a dark-blue background surmounted by six white, five-pointed stars arranged in a shallow arc. Each star is representative of an ethnic group: i.e., Albanians, Serbs, Turks, Gorani and Bosniaks.

Population:	1,827,231
Capital:	Pristina
Languages:	Albanian, Serbian
Currency:	Euro

Gjeravica, the highest mountain in Kosovo.

Medieval castle ruins in Cesis, Latvia.

Latvia

A small state lying in the Baltic region of Northern Europe, Latvia has been a unitary state since 1991, having been part of the U.S.S.R. since 1944 until independence. As an independent country, Latvia maintains strong ties with the other two Baltic states, Estonia and Lithuania. The flag was adopted in 1991 but dates back to around 1280, a popular legend associating it with a Latvian hero wrapped in a blood-stained sheet. The white band symbolizes the justice, faith, trustworthiness and honour of the people of a free Latvia.

Population:	1,985,600
Capital:	Riga
Languages:	Latvian
Currency:	Euro

Liechtenstein

The tiny principality of Liechtenstein is situated in the eastern Alps between Austria and Switzerland, and consists of the two counties of Vaduz and Schellenberg. Liechtenstein shares its currency, customs and overseas representation with Switzerland while retaining full sovereignty in other areas. The colors of the flag are

Riga, Latvia.

St. Nicholas' Church, Balzers, Liechtenstein.

traditional to the region, and it was adopted in 1921, the yellow coronet having been added to the flag in 1937. This can also be hung vertically, with the crown rotated through 90 degrees.

Population:	37,370
Capital:	Vaduz
Languages:	German
Currency:	Swiss franc

Lithuania

Lithuania is the largest Baltic state and, like Estonia and Latvia, was annexed by the U.S.S.R. in the 1940s, which was regarded by a few Western governments, notably that of the U.S.A., as an illegal occupation. Lithuania was the first of the former Soviet republics to declare itself independent and non-communist in 1990. The colors of the flag are said to symbolize Lithuania's forests and agricultural wealth, with the red representing Lithuania's flora and the blood of her martyrs. The flag is also based on the predominant colors of the national costume.

Population:	2,916,443
Capital:	Vilnius
Languages:	Lithuanian
Currency:	Euro

Luxembourg

Luxembourg is a tiny country located in central Europe and bordered by France, Belgium and Germany. It has been an independent state since 963, apart from a period in the 1800s when Luxembourg shared the same monarch with the Netherlands. The colors of the flag date back to the Grand Duke's 14th-century coat of arms, and is very similar to the Dutch flag, except that the proportions are different and the Luxembourg flag contains a paler blue.

Population:	562,958
Capital:	Luxembourg
Languages:	Letzeburgisch, French, German
Currency:	Euro

Luxembourg city.

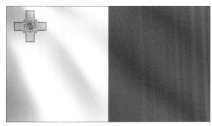

Macedonia

Once part of the former Yugoslavia, Macedonia became a unitary state in 1992. Although it is very close to the areas once engaged in civil war, Macedonia managed to avoid conflict, although there is much tension between Greece and Macedonia over the name of the country. This is because the Greeks claim an historic right to it going back to the time of the 'Greek Macedonian' Alexander the Great (356–232 B.C.), resulting in the United Nations agreeing to call the country the 'Former Yugoslav Republic of Macedonia'. The present flag shows a radiant sun on a red background, the colors borrowed from the Macedonian coat of arms, i.e., a golden lion on a red shield.

Population:	2,065,769
Capital:	Skopje
Languages:	Macedonian
Currency:	Denar

Malta

Malta is made up of three main islands and is located in the middle of the Mediterranean Sea. Malta gained independence from Britain in 1964 and the flag was adopted at this time.

Church of St. John at Kaneo, Macedonia.

Msida Parish Church, Valletta, Malta.

The colors of the flag go back a long way to the time when Malta was the headquarters of the Knights of St. John of Jerusalem, who ruled the islands from 1530 to 1898, and whose colors were red and white. The George Cross was added to the flag in 1943 to commemorate the bravery of the Maltese people during the Second World War.

Population:	425,384
Capital:	Valletta
Languages:	Maltese, English
Currency:	Euro

81

banking, finance, tourism and its famous casino. The flag was established in 1881 and repeats the colors of the Grimaldi family's coat of arms, which dates back to medieval times. The Monagasque flag is the same as that of Indonesia, but with slightly different proportions.

Moldova

Moldova is a densely populated country with many influences. It has a population made up of 75 per cent Romanians, with the remaining 25 per cent Ukrainians and Russians. It became a unitary state in 1991 after the break-up of the U.S.S.R. Moldova has expressed a wish to unite with Romania despite objections from Russia and the Ukraine, although, the people voted by a large majority in 1994 not to join Romania, deciding to remain an independent country. The flag was adopted in 1990 and is based on that of Romania. According to official description, the colors of the flag symbolize the past, present and future of Moldova.

Population:	3,555,200
Capital:	Chisinau
Languages:	Romanian
Currency:	Moldovan leu

Monaco

Monaco is the second smallest independent state in the world, being a principality ruled by the Grimaldi family since 1297. It comprises a rocky peninsula and a small stretch of coastline. Its income comes from

Population:	37,800
Capital:	Monaco-Ville
Languages:	French
Currency:	Euro

Principality of Monaco.

Montenegro

Montenegro has had a turbulent history since Roman times and its people have had a constant struggle for freedom. In relatively recent times, Montenegro was annexed to the Serb-dominated state of Yugoslavia, but when Yugoslavia broke up in the early 1990s, Montenegro did not secede, and it was not until 2006 that the loose confederation between Serbia and Montenegro broke up. The current flag dates back to before 1918 when Montenegro was a kingdom ruled by the Petrovic dynasty, whose coat of arms is now displayed at the center of the flag.

Population:	620,029
Capital:	Podgorica
Languages:	Montenegrin
Currency:	Euro

Amsterdam, Netherlands.

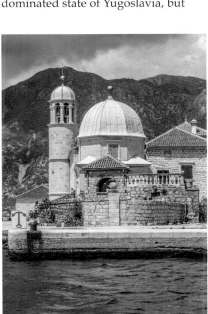

Our Lady of the Rock, Perast, Montenegro.

Netherlands

The Netherlands is a low-lying country in northern Europe. It is a highly populated country, two-fifths of which lies below sea level, making it susceptible to flooding. Large areas have been reclaimed from the sea and for centuries inundation has been prevented by the construction of dykes and sand dunes along the coast. The flag dates back to 1630, when it was first adopted, and is one of the oldest flags in Europe. At the end of the 16th century, the Netherlands was part of the Spanish Empire. The fight for independence was led by Prince William of Orange, of the House of Nassau-Dillenburg, who was assassinated by a Roman Catholic in 1584. The first flag was based on his livery.

Population:	16,900,100
Capital:	Amsterdam
Languages:	Dutch
Currency:	Euro

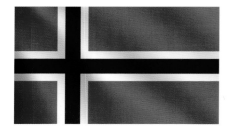

Norway

Located on the Scandinavian Peninsula, Norway's sparse population is concentrated mainly in the southern part of the country. Norway's flag dates from 1898, although it was used by merchants from 1821. The off-center cross is typical of the flags of other Scandinavian countries and is based on a legend which describes King Waldemar II as having seen a vision of a white cross in the sky before the Battle of Lyndanisse in 1219. The flag is essentially the same as that of the Danes, but with the addition of the blue cross, the color scheme representing Norwegian nationalism.

Population:	5,165,802
Capital:	Oslo
Languages:	Norwegian
Currency:	Krone

Poland

Poland's position in Europe goes a long way to explain its complex and varied history. With constant invasions from neighboring countries, it has been partitioned several times and re-founded twice in this century. Poland was the first satellite country of the Soviet Union to bring down its communist regime, which encouraged many other Eastern European countries to follow suit. The colors of the flag derive from those of the Polish coat of arms (a white eagle on a red field) which dates back to the 13th century. The flag, using red and white, was first used in 1919. Since 1989 when anti-communists took over, it has been a popular notion that the colors stand for peace (white) and socialism (red).

Population:	38,484,000
Capital:	Warsaw
Languages:	Polish
Currency:	Złoty

An aurora borealis display, Norway.

The re-built old town of Warsaw, Poland.

Portugal

Portugal is situated on the Atlantic coastline of the Iberian peninsula. Important for its maritime history, it was the first European country to send a ship around the world. Portugal joined the European Union in 1986, but remains comparatively poor in relation

Corvinesti Castle, Hunedoara, Romania.

to other European countries. The flag dates from 1910 when Portugal became a republic, with red symbolizing the revolution that took place and green standing for hope and the sea. The central shield dates back to the 12th century, created when Alfonso I defeated five Moorish kings at the Battle of Ourique. The coat of arms is set on an armillary sphere, a nautical instrument which recalls the time of the Portuguese maritime voyages of exploration.

Romania

Dominated by the Carpathian Mountains and the lower plains of the Danube, Romania has a variety of landscapes. The country became communist in 1946, with elections following in 1992 following the collapse of the Ceausescu regime. The colors of the flag are those of Moldavia and Wallachia, the two provinces which had united in 1861 to become Romania, the Wallachian colors being blue and yellow and the Moldavian colors blue and red. Before the downfall of communism in Romania, the flag displayed the communist arms within the central yellow stripe.

Palace of Sintra, Portugal.

Population:	10,477,800
Capital:	Lisbon
Languages:	Portuguese
Currency:	Euro

Population:	19,942,642
Capital:	Bucharest
Languages:	Romanian
Currency:	Leu

Russia

The Russian Federation is a collection of republics and the largest in the world, with a wide variety of landscapes and climates. The Communist system was established in 1917 when the tsars were overthrown. The Russian Federation was part of the U.S.S.R. until 1991, when many of its republics broke away to form the Commonwealth of Independent States, with the Russian Federation being the largest member. In December 1991 the national flag of the Soviet Union (hammer and sickle on red) was removed from the topmost tower of the Kremlin, and the old Russian flag was hoisted, which dates back to the 17th century as a mercantile flag of Russian vessels, later regarded as bearing the 'pan-Slavic' colors.

Population:	146,267,288
Capital:	Moscow
Languages:	Russian
Currency:	Ruble

San Marino

San Marino is one of the oldest states in Europe and the world's smallest republic. The country lies completely within the territory of Italy and has been independent since 885. Tourism is the main activity, but there is some farming and manufacturing, mainly of craft goods. The flag is a simple bicolor symbolizing snowy mountains and a blue sky, colors which derive from the country's coat of arms which dates back to 1787.

Population:	32,789
Capital:	San Marino
Languages:	Italian
Currency:	Euro

St. Basil's Cathedral, Moscow, Russia.

Belgrade, Serbia.

Serbia

Serbia is a fertile but largely mountainous country bordering on Croatia, Hungary, Romania, Bulgaria, Macedonia, Albania, Montenegro and Bosnia & Herzegovina. It was one of six republics which broke up in the

1990s. Serbia and Montenegro remained part of the former Yugoslavia until 2006 when Montenegro split from Serbia. The Serbian flag is a tricolor composed of the pan-Slavic colors of red, blue and white, the red signifying sacrifice and war, the blue nature, land, water and sky and the white freedom. The coat of arms is that of the Obrenovic dynasty dating from 1882 to 1903.

Population:	7,146,759
Capital:	Belgrade
Languages:	Serbo-Croatian
Currency:	Serbian dinar

Lake Strbske Pleso, High Tatras, Slovakia.

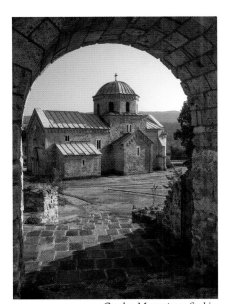

Gradac Monastery, Serbia.

Slovakia

Slovakia was once part of the former Czechoslovakia, but in 1993 broke away amicably and the two new states of the Czech Republic and Slovakia continue to maintain close links with one another. The flag shows the pan-Slavic colors, with the state arms superimposed. This is composed of a red background and a blue mountain with three peaks, with a white double cross at its center. The flag dates from 1848, but was officially adopted in January 1993.

Population:	5,421,349
Capital:	Bratislava
Languages:	Slovak
Currency:	Euro

Slovenia

Slovenia is situated in the northern part of the former Yugoslavia. It first became an independent state in 1991 when it seceded from Yugoslavia after a brief period of civil war which was less bloody than that suffered by Croatia. The flag displays the pan-Slavic colors of white, blue and red, and also shows the Slovenian state arms; these show a blue field and white mountain with three peaks representing the country's terrain, and two blue wavy lines passing through its foot symbolizing the country's two main rivers, the Sava and Drava.

Population:	2,066,451
Capital:	Ljubljana
Languages:	Slovenian
Currency:	Euro

Spain

Spain is a large European country lying close to northern Africa. The country has varied landscapes with large areas of scrub, forests and mountains. Spain became united in 1579 when different independent kingdoms merged together, although the colors of the flag date from the 12th century and were those of the old kingdom of Aragon. Today's flag dates back to 1938 and the time of the civil war. The 'excess width' of the yellow band is the result of a maritime requirement to make the Spanish flag more visible at sea.

Population:	46,464,053
Capital:	Madrid
Languages:	Spanish
Currency:	Euro

Plaza de España, Seville, Spain.

Toledo, Spain.

Sweden

Lying on the eastern half of the Scandinavian peninsula, Sweden is a country of forests, fertile plains and lakes, much of which was shaped during the Ice Age. Sweden is one of the oldest kingdoms in Europe. It joined the European Union in 1995. The colors of the flag were taken from an ancient state coat of arms dating from the 14th century, although there is evidence to suggest that it was used from 1449 onwards. The off-center cross, common to all Scandinavian countries, derives from the flag of Denmark.

Population:	9,760,142
Capital:	Stockholm
Languages:	Swedish
Currency:	Krona

Switzerland

Switzerland is a mainly alpine country, with mountains covering 60 per cent of its area. Despite the four main languages of French, German, Italian and Romansch, Switzerland is a stable, united country enjoying high living standards. The Swiss flag dates from the 14th century and was used in the struggle for liberation from the Holy Roman Empire. Apart from the flag of the Vatican City, the Swiss flag is the only one that is completely square. The reverse form of the Swiss flag became that of the Red Cross, founded in 1864 in honour of the Swiss philanthropist Henri Dunant.

Population:	8,211,700
Capital:	Bern
Languages:	German, French, Italian, Romansch
Currency:	Swiss franc

Old Town (Gamla stan), Stockholm, Sweden.

Oberhofen Castle on Lake Thun, Switzerland

Transnistria

Transnistria (official name Pridnestrovian Moldavian Republic) is a part of Moldova that declared its independence in 1990, resulting in a civil war that lasted until 1992. Transnistria has not been recognized by any United Nations member but maintains its functional autonomy with military and other support from Russia. The flag of the Moldavian Soviet Socialist Republic served as the republic's flag until the dissolution of the Soviet Union in 1991. When Moldova became independent, some places in Transnistria refused to fly the new Moldovan flag and continued to fly the flag of the Soviet Union. Continued use of the flag of the former Moldavian SSR was popular and it was officially reintroduced as the flag of Transnistria in 2000. Confusingly, despite the flag and coat of arms, Transnistria is not a Communist state.

Population:	505,153
Capital:	Tiraspol
Languages:	Russian, Moldovan, Ukranian
Currency:	Transnistrian ruble

Ukraine

The Ukraine is the largest country within the boundaries of Europe and is made up of fertile uplands with the Carpathian Mountains in the west, the north of the country made up of lowlands. A great deal of the nation's agricultural land was ruined in the 1986 Chernobyl disaster when radioactive fall-out spread across the country. The Ukraine broke away from the former Soviet Union in 1991. The flag dates back to 1848, the colors having been used on a Ukrainian coat of arms. Originally used from 1918 to 1920, the flag was re-adopted in 1991.

Population:	42,895,704
Capital:	Kiev
Languages:	Ukrainian
Currency:	Hryvnia

St. Michael's Monastery, Kiev, Ukraine

United Kingdom

The United Kingdom of Great Britain and Northern Ireland is made up of England, Scotland, Wales, Northern

Stonehenge, Wiltshire, England.

Ireland and many off-shore islands. The country is situated on the westernmost edge of Europe and despite being situated in a northerly position, has a temperate climate due to the North Atlantic Drift. The flag dates from 1603 and combines the crosses of St. George of England and St. Andrew of Scotland. The Irish cross of St. Patrick was added in 1801 to the flag as we know it today.

Population: 64,800,000
Capital: London
Languages: English
Currency: Pound sterling

Houses of Parliament and Big Ben, London, England.

Divisions of the United Kingdom

Wales

Northern Ireland

England

Scotland

Eilean Donan Castle, Scotland.

Dunluce Castle, Antrim, Northern Ireland.

Isle of Man

Guernsey

Jersey

Great Laxey Wheel with viaduct, Isle of Man.

Tryfan Mountain, Snowdonia National Park, Wales.

Mont Orgueil Castle, Gorey, Jersey, Channel Islands.

Vatican City

The Vatican City is the smallest independent state in the world. It lies within central Rome, and was created in 1929, the year Pope Pius XI signed the Lateran Treaty with Italy, creating a new independent state governed by the Holy See. The Vatican flag is modelled on that of the earlier Papal States dating from 1825. It bears the emblem of the triple tiara of the Popes and features the keys of Heaven (according to the Gospel of Matthew 16:19), given by Jesus Christ to St. Peter, with the result that the popes are regarded as the successors of Peter, the first Pope.

Population:	839
Languages:	Italian
Currency:	Euro

St. Peter's Basilica, Vatican City.

CHAPTER FOUR
ASIA

Daigo-ji Shingon Buddhist temple, Fushimi-ku, Japan.

Hindu Kush mountain range, Afghanistan.

Abkhazia

Abkhazia is a partially recognized state which considers itself independent of Georgia, although Georgia disputes this, even though Abkhazia is legally governed by the Government of the Autonomous Republic of Abkhazia. The flag was first issued in 1991 and was officially adopted on 23 July 1992, the design of the red canton having been based on the banner of the medieval Abkhazian Kingdom, the open right hand meaning 'Hello to Friends! Stop to Enemies'. The seven stars in the canton have since been reinterpreted to correspond with the seven historial regions of the country: Sadzen, Bzyp, Gumaa, Abzhywa, Samurzaqan, Dal-Tsabal and Pskhuy-Aibja. The seven green and white stripes represent peace and tolerance.

Simon the Zealot Monastery, New Athos, Abkhazia.

Population:	240,705
Capital:	Sukhumi
Languages:	Abkhaz, Russian
Currency:	Ruble

Afghanistan

A landlocked country, Afghanistan has had a turbulent history, and the fact that the Khyber Pass is not only the gateway to India, but also the back door to Russia, has caused numerous conflicts. The Soviet invasion of 1979–1988, and the following civil war, lasted into the 1990s. War broke out again in 2001, when the U.S.

invaded Afghanistan, supported by its allies and later NATO, following the terrorist attack on the World Trade Center in New York, the aim being to dismantle the terrorist group al-Qaeda. The current Afghani flag contains three solid colors, black, red and green, representing different pages in the history of Afghanistan. The black represents the 19th century era, when Afghanistan was occupied and did not have independence, the red signifies the blood shed in the struggle for independence, with the green being the color of Islam and representing the era when independence was achieved as well as hope and prosperity for the future. In the center is the classical emblem of Afghanistan, featuring a mosque with its mihrab facing Mecca.

Population:	26,556,800
Capital:	Kabul
Languages:	Pashto, Dari
Currency:	Afgháni

Armenia

Armenia is a physically hostile, mountainous country, landlocked between unfriendly neighbors and situated in an earthquake zone. The economy is weak with little industry, although Armenia successfully produces tobacco and wine. In 1991, Armenia became independent from the U.S.S.R., although it had been the first to be established in the 8th century B.C. as an independent kingdom. This flag, first used between 1812 and 1822, was re-adopted on 24 August 1990, with the red representing the blood shed in the past, blue the land of Armenia, and orange the courage of the people.

Population:	3,013,900
Capital:	Yerevan
Languages:	Armenian
Currency:	Dram

Sevanavank (Sevan Monastery), Lake Sevan, Armenia.

Azerbaijan

Azerbaijan is flanked by the Caspian Sea and the Caucasus mountains. It became independent in 1991, at the time of the breakdown of the U.S.S.R. Azerbaijan has a history of conflict with Armenia over the predominantly Armenian enclave of Nagorno-Karabakh, that led to was heavy fighting in the late 1980s and 1990s. It is a land rich in natural resources with the potential to develop a successful economy in the future. Azerbaijan means 'Land of Flames', which comes from the fact that in many areas natural gas seeps up directly from the ground. The flag first came into being on 5 February 1991. The blue represents the sky, the red is for freedom and the green for the land and the Islamic religion. The crescent also represents Islam. There are eight ethnic groups in Azerbaijan and this is reflected in the eight points of the star.

Population:	9,611,700
Capital:	Baku
Languages:	Azerbaijani
Currency:	Manat

Bahrain

Situated off the coast of Saudi Arabia, 35 islands make up the country of Bahrain in the southern Persian Gulf. Bahrain led the way in oil exportation which began in the 1930s. It is ruled by a hereditary amir, and resumed its independent status in 1971. Its flag is based on the one used by several of the Gulf states, deriving from those of the Kharidjite sect of Islam. Originally, the flag was plain red, with white borders added to signify acceptance of the General Treaty with the United Kingdom. The serration of the vertical stripe also came later in 1932, for which the reason is not clear, although it may have been to differentiate it

Baku Boulevard, Baku, Azerbaijan.

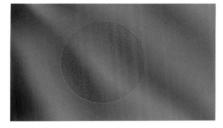

Bangladesh

Once described as 'golden Bengal', Bangladesh is mainly lowland and is home to the huge delta of the Ganges and Brahmaputra rivers. It is an area that frequently floods, making life very difficult for its inhabitants. Once East Pakistan, Bangladesh was established in 1971. It is one of the world's poorest countries and has a rapidly growing and dense population which hinders economic growth. The green background is said to represent the fertility of the land as well as Islam and the red disc commemorates the blood shed in the struggle for freedom.

Population:	158,245,000
Capital:	Dhaka
Languages:	Bengali
Currency:	Taka

Financial district, Manama, Bahrain.

from the flags of its neighbors or to represent the five pillars of Islam.

Population:	1,316,500
Capital:	Manama
Languages:	Arabic
Currency:	Bahrain dinar

Dhaka, Bangladesh.

Trashi Chhoe Dzong, Thimphu, Bhutan.

Bhutan

Bhutan is a kingdom lying in the eastern Himalayas between India and Tibet. It is a remote, rural, country and dependent on agriculture, producing mainly rice and maize. The wingless

dragon grasping four jewels is Bhutan's national symbol. In the local language Bhutan is known as Druk-Yul, which means 'Land of the Thunder Dragon'. The two colors of the triangles have varied over the years, but the saffron yellow stands for the king's authority and the orange-red for Buddhist spiritual power.

Population:	759,890
Capital:	Thimphu
Languages:	Dzongkha
Currency:	Ngultrum

Brunei

Brunei is a tropical country made up of two enclaves bordering on Malaysia. It was a British protectorate from 1888 to 1984. The Sultan of Brunei, reputed to be the richest man in the world, now rules by ancient hereditary rights. The yellow background to the flag represents royalty in the Malay world. The black

and white stripes stand for the Sultan's two advisers, which suggests that he does not have total power. The arms were added in 1959. The inscription on the crescent is 'Always serve with the guidance of God', the crescent itself symbolizing Islam. Under the crescent is a scroll bearing the legend 'Brunei, City of Peace', the open hands indicating the goodwill of the government.

Population:	393,372
Capital:	Bandar Seri Begawan
Languages:	Malay
Currency:	Brunei dollar

Sultan Omar Ali Saifuddin Mosque, Bandar Seri Begawan, Brunei.

Taktshang Goemba (Tiger's Nest Monastery), Bhutan.

109

Royal Palace complex, Phnom Penh, Cambodia.

Cambodia

With a tropical monsoon climate, three-quarters of Cambodia is forested. After French rule, from 1863 to 1954, Cambodia finally achieved independence, although the dictatorship of the Khmer Rouge and civil war has left Cambodia in an impoverished state. Following UN supervision, elections in 1993 introduced a government of national unity. Red is the traditional color of Cambodia as well as being associated with communism and revolution. The icon is that of Angkor Wat, the main temple dating from the 12th century, with the blue symbolizing water, which is a particularly important resource to the Cambodians.

Population:	15,405,157
Capital:	Phnom Penh
Languages:	Khmer
Currency:	Riel

Angkor Wat, Cambodia.

The Great Wall, near Beijing, China.

China

China is a hugely populated country with 20 per cent of the world's people living here; it is the world's third largest nation. China became a republic in 1912. The following years were to be turbulent and there

The Terracotta Army, Lintong District, Xian, Shaanxi province, China.

followed a long period of anarchy. Eventually, in 1949, the triumphant communists declared a People's Republic of China in October and this is when the flag was introduced. The red and yellow are the traditional colors of China. Red is also the color of communism, with the larger star representing the ideology's guiding light. The smaller stars represent the four levels of Chinese society: the peasantry, the workers, the bourgeoisie and those capitalists who would participate in the ongoing revolution.

Population:	1,369,550,000
Capital:	Beijing
Languages:	Chinese and Yuan variants, with local languages
Currency:	Yuan

Shanghai, China.

Cyprus

An island nation in the north-east Mediterranean, Cyprus is small but strategically placed. Since becoming independent from Britain in 1960, Cyprus has continued to witness the struggle between Turkish and Greek Cypriots and the island is still divided into two opposed states, although that in the north is recognized solely by Turkey. The white background to the flag, and the two olive branches, are meant to signify peace, with the map of the island representing a neutral portrayal of the country. Sadly, the flag seems to represents hope rather than reality.

Population:	1,172,458
Capital:	Nicosia
Languages:	Greek, Turkish
Currency:	Euro

East Timor

East Timor is located in the eastern part of Timor, having became independent from Indonesia in May 2002. Since then, it has struggled economically, relying heavily on foreign money. Today, East Timor has grown famous for its sought-after

Kyrenia harbour, Cyprus.

Lighthouse, Dili, East Timor.

arabica coffee beans, noted for their distinctive character, and some 50,000 people work in this industry. East Timor has great potential for tourism and it is hoped that this will further boost the economy as the country becomes more established. The flag's black triangle represents a period of 400 years of colonization. The red is for blood shed during its fight for independence and the white for peace. The five-pointed star represents hope for the nation's future.

Population: 1,212,107
Capital: Dili
Languages: Tetum
Currency: U.S. dollar

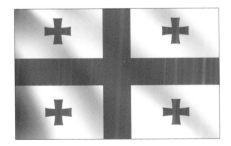

Georgia

Georgia is positioned between Russia and Turkey. It is the land of the legendary Golden Fleece of Greek mythology, and has a fascinating history and culture. Georgia became

part of the Russian Empire in 1800, and in 1990 became independent, following the Baltic States in leaving the former U.S.S.R. The current flag was originally used by the Georgian patriotic movement following independence, although it wasn't until the late 1990s that the design started to become accepted as 'the Georgian historical national flag'. It was finally adopted by Parliament on 14 January 2004 and was endorsed by Presidential Decree No. 31 on 25 January. The flag of Georgia is white,

with a large red cross centered on it. In each of the four white rectangles, created by the cross, are small red crosses. The large cross is known as St. George's cross, the small crosses are said to represent the five holy wounds suffered by Christ during his crucifixion.

Population: 4,490,500
Capital: Tbilisi
Languages: Georgian
Currency: Lari

Adishi, Upper Svaneti, Georgia.

India

The subcontinent of India encompasses the world's seventh largest country. Being so large, India has a wide variety of landscapes and climates. Britain established a colony in the 1800s and its rule lasted until 1947 when India became independent, at which time it was subdivided into Hindu India and Muslim Pakistan. The non-violent freedom campaign was led by Mahatma Gandhi. The saffron color of the flag represents the Hindus, the green the Muslims and the white is for peace. The wheel is an ancient symbol – the Dharma Chakra, or 'wheel of law'. The flag evolved during the struggle for independence.

Population:	1,270,444,000
Capital:	New Delhi
Languages:	Hindi
Currency:	Rupee

Jal Mahal (Water Palace), Man Sagar Lake, Jaipur, India.

Gadi Sagar (Gadisar) Lake, Jaisalmer, Rajasthan, India.

Bromo Tengger Semeru National Park, East Java, Indonesia.

Indonesia

Indonesia consists of 13,700 islands, some of which are volcanic, and also extends into part of western New Guinea, which was acquired in 1963. The islands are mountainous and temperatures are high throughout the year. From the 1500s, the Dutch dominated the country and it was in 1949, after a four-year struggle, that independence was achieved. The white band of the flag represents purity and the red stands for gallantry and freedom.

Population:	255,461,700
Capital:	Jakarta
Languages:	Bahasa Indonesian
Currency:	Rupiah

Iran

Iran was known as Persia before 1935. It borders the Caspian Sea in the north and has a varied landscape, including mountains, deserts and high plateaux. Iran was ruled by its shah until the monarchy was overthrown by the revolution in 1978 and the nation became an Islamic Republic under the Ayatollah Ruhollah Khomeini. The flag dates back to 1910, adopted in its current form after the shah had been expelled. The emblem in the centre is a sword surrounded by crescents which represents Islamic values and Allah (God). Along the edge of each stripe, repeated 22 times, are the words 'Allah Akbar' (God is Great).

Population:	78,297,700
Capital:	Tehran
Languages:	Persian
Currency:	Rial

Limestone islands in a remote lagoon in northern Raja Ampat, Indonesia.,

Iraq

The famous Tigris and Euphrates rivers make up the fertile crescent of Iraq, a country that was under strong British influence from 1916 when it was governed almost as a colony. The kingdom was ruled by the Hashemite dynasty until 1958 when it became a Republic, with control was taken by the Baathists in 1968. By 1979, Saddam Hussein had become president, and the Iran-Iraq war of the 1980s devastated Iraq. Further wars broke out in 1990 and in 2003, when U.S.-led forces invaded, disposing of the Baathists and creating a subsequent power vacuum. Today, Iraq is still in a state or turmoil. Dating from 2008, the Iraqi flag is a tricolor of red, black and white, with green Arabic text showing the Takbir, meaning 'God is Great', along the white central panel. The colors derive from the Arab Liberation flag and represent oppression (black), overcome through bloody struggle (red), and replaced by a bright future (white).

Population:	36,004,522
Capital:	Baghdad
Languages:	Arabic
Currency:	Iraqi dinar

Israel

The State of Israel was created in 1948 and marked the return of the Jews to their homeland. Israel is an arid country with half its territory covered by desert. The people of Israel have worked very hard to reclaim swamplands and to irrigate the dry areas to make fertile farmland. The flag was designed in America in 1891, in the early days of the Zionist movement, the blue stripes representing the traditional colors of the Jewish prayer cloth. The Star of David in the center is a centuries-old symbol of the Jewish faith.

Population:	8,345,00
Capital:	Jerusalem
Languages:	Hebrew, Arabic
Currency:	Sheqel

Castle of Erbil, Iraq.

The Old City with the Western Wall and Temple Mount, Jerusalem, Israel.

Mount Fuji, Japan.

Japan

Japan is an archipelago, the four main islands being Hokkaido, Honshu, Shikoku and Kyushu, situated in a geologically unstable zone where there are frequent volcanic eruptions. Japan is one of the oldest monarchies in the world and its emperor is the ceremonial head of state of Japan's system of constitutional monarchy. Historically, the emperor is the highest authority of the Shinto religion and his family claim descent from the sun-goddess Amaterasuthe. The name Japan means 'Land of the Rising Sun', and this is represented in the flag, the redness of the disc denoting passion and sincerity, the whiteness honesty and purity.

Population:	126,910,000
Capital:	Tokyo
Languages:	Japanese
Currency:	Yen

Jordan

Jordan lies east of Israel in an area of mostly desert with a small stretch of Red Sea coastline. After the First World War, Jordan, then known as Transjordan, was passed from Turkish to British control, the country becoming fully independent as Jordan

Tokyo, Japan.

Petra, Jordan.

in 1946. The flag is composed of the pan-Arab colors. The black, white and green represents the three tribes which led the Arab Revolt against the Turks in 1917, with red being the color of the Hussein dynasty. The star is a reminder of the first seven verses of the Koran.

Population:	6,723,360
Capital:	Amman
Languages:	Arabic
Currency:	Jordanian dinar

Astana, Kazakhstan.

Kazakhstan

Kazakhstan is a very large country composed mainly of vast steppes and desert. The weather is very hot in summer and very cold in winter, this being a typical extreme continental

Zenkov Cathedral, Almaty, Kazakhstan.

Arch of Triumph, Pyongyang, North Korea.

climate. Kazakhstan has been dominated by Russian regimes over the years, but was a leader in the breakaway of republics into the new Commonwealth of Independent States in 1991. Adopted in June 1992, the new flag has a blue background representing the skies and the golden sun, the soaring eagle symbolizing freedom. The vertical strip on the left of the flag is ornamentation.

Population:	17,458,500
Capital:	Almaty (Alma-Ata)
Languages:	Kazakh
Currency:	Tenge

Korea, North

Covering the northern part of the Korean Peninsula, the People's Democratic Republic of North Korea is largely mountainous and the climate can be harsh. After the Second World War, the country of Korea was split into two: North and South Korea. The north was influenced by the Soviet Union and a Stalinist government took over. The country is now very isolated and there is constant fear that war with South Korea will break out over territory. The flag not only shows traditional Korean design and colors, but it also bears the red star indicative of a communist regime.

Population:	25,155,00
Capital:	Pyongyang
Languages:	Korean
Currency:	Won

Korea, South

South Korea covers the southern part of the Korean Peninsula. It is a highly populated country and the landscape is mostly highland. After the partitioning of Korea, South Korea was established as a democracy. The economy grew rapidly and Korea became a significant exporter of manufactured goods. The flag was adopted in 1950, the central feature being the yin-yang symbol, which in Buddhism signifies nature's opposing forces. The white background is for peace and unity and the black symbols stand for the seasons, the points of the compass and the sun, moon, earth and sky.

Population:	51,342,881
Capital:	Seoul
Languages:	Korean
Currency:	Won

Kuwait

Kuwait is an emirate lying in the Arabian Gulf. Since 1756 it has been ruled by the al-Sabah family. It is largely desert and gets little rain. Kuwait was a British protectorate from 1914 to 1961 when it finally gained independence. It was occupied by Iraq in 1990 but a multinational force expelled the Iraqis in 1991. War damage, including the burning of oil wells, was extensive. The flag, dating from independence, features the four pan-Arab colors signifying unity.

Population:	3,268,431
Capital:	Kuwait
Languages:	Arabic
Currency:	Dinar

Gyeongbokgung Palace, Seoul, South Korea.

Kuwait City.

Kyrgyzstan

Kyrgyzstan is a remote, isolated mountainous country in Central Asia. Independence was achieved at the time of the breakdown of the U.S.S.R. in 1991, but there are disputes over its north-western border with China. The country has strong links with neighboring Kazakhstan. The flag was first adopted in March 1992, the symbol in the center being a yurt, as seen from above, this being a temporary house of animal skins lashed over a circular wooden frame, symbolizing the nation's nomadic way of life. The rays of the sun, surrounding the yurt, represent the 40 tribes of Kyrgyzstan.

Population:	5,915,300
Capital:	Bishkek
Languages:	Kyrgyz
Currency:	Som

Tien Shan Mountains, Kyrgyzstan.

Tien Shan, Kyrgyzstan.

The Song river, Vang Vieng, Laos.

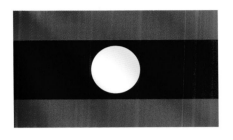

Laos

Laos is located in South-East Asia, this being a landlocked, narrow country dependent on the Mekong river for transportation. Laos was once part of Indochina and ruled by the French. Independence was granted in 1954, followed by 20 years of bitter civil war, after which the communists took power. The country remains very poor. The flag was adopted by the communists in 1975. The white disc is the moon and signifies the well-being of the people, the blue stripe representing the Mekong river. The red strip on either side symbolizes the blood that was shed during the fight for independence.

Population:	6,802,000
Capital:	Vientiane
Languages:	Lao
Currency:	Kip

Lebanon

Bordering the Mediterranean Sea, Lebanon is a mountainous country. Lebanon has been influenced by French culture and, indeed, was ruled by the French from 1918 to 1944. After the country gained its independence, there was a period of 30 years of calm until civil war broke out in 1975.

Paddyfield, Vang Vieng, Laos.

Roman Temple of Jupiter, Baalbek, Lebanon.

Muslims, Christians and Druses fought for control and the result is a war-torn land, with a situation that has been complicated by Israeli occupation of southern Lebanon. Officially, the civil war is over, but armed factions still control different areas of the country. The flag, adopted on independence, has the Cedar of Lebanon in the center, which has been the traditional symbol of the country since biblical times.

Population:	4,104,000
Capital:	Beirut
Languages:	Arabic
Currency:	Lebanese pound

Malaysia

The present Federation of Malaysia comprises 13 states, partly in Malaya and partly in Borneo. The vegetation is rain forest in the lower areas, with montane on the higher ground. The official religion is Islam, although there are many ethnic groups with varying religions, which has caused tension in recent times. This version of the flag was first flown in 1963, although an earlier form dates back to 1950, the 14 red and white stripes representing the 13 states and the federal territory of Kuala Lumpur. These stripes are said to date back to the 13th century. The crescent and star represent Islam. The blue symbolizes Malaysia's British links and the yellow the states that are sultanates.

Population:	30,566,200
Capital:	Kuala Lumpur
Languages:	Bahasa Malay
Currency:	Ringgit

Petronas Towers, Kuala Lumpur, Malaysia.

Maldives

The Maldives are an archipelago of around 2,000 islands, the word 'Maldives', in fact, meaning 'Thousand Islands'. The islands are scattered in a line in the Indian Ocean south-west of India. They were a British protectorate until 1965, when independence was established. The early flag of the Maldives was plain red, reflecting the culture of the numerous Arab traders who operated among the many islands. The later addition of the Islamic green panel, and the crescent thereon, could also be attributed to the Arabian influence.

Population:	341,256
Capital:	Malé
Languages:	Divehi
Currency:	Rufiyaa

Mongolia

Sparsely populated, with the arid Gobi Desert making up 25 per cent of the country and with high mountains to the north and west, Mongolia is a large country, influenced by both the Soviet Union and China. Mongolia was one of the very first communist

Valley of Karakorum, Mongolia.

Myanmar

Until 1991, the Republic of the Union of Myanmar was known as Burma. Adjacent to the Malay Peninsula, the country is situated in a great structural depression. To the west are the mountains of the Arakan Yoma, and to the east the Shan Platea, with 60 per cent of the country covered in forest. The people speak Burmese, a language related to Tibetan, and the population also includes many minority hill peoples. Myanmar was annexed by Britain in 1895 and finally became independent in 1948, leaving the Commonwealth. The flag of Myanmar was adopted on 21 October 2010 to replace the socialist flag, its design comprising three stripes of yellow, green and red, horizontally positioned, with a large, white five-pointed star in the center. The meaning behind the colors is that of solidarity, peace and tranquillity.

Population:	51,419,420
Capital:	Yangon (Rangoon)
Languages:	Burmese
Currency:	Kyat

states, declaring itself a people's republic as early a 1924. In 1946, its independence was guaranteed by a treaty with the Soviet Union. The flag dates from 1940, the blue being the country's national color and the red reflecting the communist past. The Golden Soyonbo is a Buddhist symbol, representing freedom, the flame standing for the promise of prosperity and progress.

Population:	3,015,755
Capital:	Ulan Bator
Languages:	Mongolian
Currency:	Tugrik

Ananda Temple, Bagan, Myanmar.

Nepal

The Kingdom of Nepal is located in the heartland of the Himalayas and is the home of the famous Gurkha people who have dominated the country since the 16th century. The most striking feature of the Nepalese flag is its shape: this version of the flag dates from 1962, when the two triangular pennants were joined together. The crescent and moon represent the Ráná family, which once held prime ministerial office and control of the nation, the sun symbol representing the country's royal family. Prior to 1962, both symbols carried human faces.

Population:	28,037,904
Capital:	Kathmandu
Languages:	Nepali
Currency:	Nepalese rupee

Oman

Oman is located on the south-eastern coast of the Persian Gulf. Since 1744, it has been ruled by the Sa'idi family, which also ruled at one time in Zanzibar and East Africa. The country has huge natural gas deposits and has been developing rapidly since the 1970s. The flag dates back to 1970, when it replaced the plain red flag typical of the Gulf states. The emblem, however, is traditional, and shows a dagger fastened over a pair of crossed sabres. Red is the nation's color, the white being symbolic of the traditional Imam of Oman, the green being for the mountainous regions of the country.

Population:	4,161,705
Capital:	Muscat
Languages:	Arabic
Currency:	Omani rial

Annapurna South, Himalayas, Nepal.

The old town of Muscat, Oman.

Nanga Parbat Mountain, North Pakistan.

Pakistan

Pakistan lies to the north-west of India and became separated from it in 1947. Created by the Muslim League, Pakistan is predominately a Muslim state, although there are other religions in the country. East Pakistan (Bangladesh) broke way from the west in 1971 and Kashmir remains a disputed region between India and Pakistan. Civil war, and the fear of Indian military intervention, have seen Pakistan ruled by the military for much of its history. Nawaz Sharif is the current leader. The Muslim League created the flag and it dates back to 1906, the green flag, with the white crescent and star, being traditional to many Islamic flags. The white stripe signifies Pakistan's tolerance towards other religions.

Population:	189,644,00
Capital:	Islamabad
Languages:	Urdu
Currency:	Pakistan rupee

University of Peshawar, Pakistan.

Palestine

(West Bank and Gaza)

Palestine has had a long and turbulent history of imposed rule and occupation that is still unresolved. The current flag was first used by the Arab National Movement in 1917, readopted in 1948, then endorsed by the PLO in 1964. The flag is a tricolor of three equal horizontal stripes. Green represents the land of Palestine, red the blood shed in the fight for independence, black for mourning and white for peace.

Population:	4,682,467
Capital:	Ramallah
Languages:	Palestinian Arabic
Currency:	Israeli new sheqel

Bethlehem, Palestine.

Population: 101,365,600
Capital: Manila
Languages: English, Filipino
Currency: Philippine peso

Philippines

The Philippines comprise over 7,000 islands, the two main ones, Luzon and Mindanao, dominating much of the total area. The Philippines were ruled by the Spanish for 300 years until 1898 when the islands were ceded to the U.S.A. In 1986, the corrupt regime of President Marcos was overthrown and Cory Aquino took office. Benigno S. Aquino III is the current leader. The first official use of the flag was in 1946, when the country became independent from the U.S.A., although the flag had been designed by nationalists in exile while the country was still controlled by Spain. Based on the stars and stripes, the eight rays of the sun represent the island's provinces which declared independence from the Spanish, the three stars symbolizing the three main island groups, with the white for purity and peace, the blue for idealism and the red for gallantry.

Coron, Busuanga Island, Palawan, Philippines.

Makati City, Metro Manila, Philippines.

Qatar

Qatar is situated on a barren peninsula in the Arabian Gulf adjacent to the United Arab Emirates. Much of its wealth comes from oil and gas, although it has recently started to diversify. Before 1820, many Arab countries flew the plain red flags of the Kharidjite sect of Islam and this was how Qatar's flag originated, with the maroon color of the flag said to derive from the effect of sunlight on a red flag. The white was added at the request of the British in 1820 to signify peace in the waters surrounding the country. The flag also has unusual proportions, in that its width is more than twice its height.

Population:	2,334,029
Capital:	Doha
Languages:	Arabic
Currency:	Rial

Saudi Arabia

Saudi Arabia is the largest country in the Middle East, although the vast majority of it is desert. The country has huge reserves of oil which produce great wealth. Dating from 1906, the flag is based on the country's Muslim religion, the meaning of the inscription being, 'There is no God but Allah, and Mohammed is the Prophet of Allah'. The sword stands for the Sa'udi family's determination to impose their rule on Arabia, while the green background commemorates the Prophet Mohammed.

Population:	31,521,418
Capital:	Riyadh
Languages:	Arabic
Currency:	Saudi Arabian riyal

Petrochemical plant, Saudi Arabia.

Chinatown and downtown Singapore.

Singapore

Singapore comprises one main island with another 54 smaller ones situated off the southern coast of the Malay peninsula. Singapore was a British colony from 1867 to 1959 when the country attained self-government. For two years, between 1963 and 1965, Singapore was part of the Federation of Malaysia, until 1965, when it became fully independent. Adopted in 1959, the Singapore flag has the traditional Malaysian colors of red and white. The white is as ever for peace, virtue and purity and the red for the universal fellowship of mankind. The five stars stand for the five ideals on which the state is founded: peace, progress, justice, quality and democracy, with the crescent representing the new and growing nation.

Population:	5,469,700
Capital:	Singapore
Languages:	Chinese, English, Malay, Tamil
Currency:	Singapore dollar

Lakeside monastery, Tskhinvali, South Ossetia.

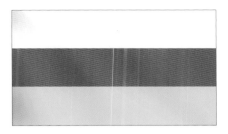

South Ossetia

South Ossetia is legally part of Georgia, but had an autonomous status until 1990 when the Georgian authorities abolished its status, which led to a revolt when Ossetians fought to unite with North Ossetia in Russia. Since then, Russian peacekeepers have been deployed to keep the situation under control. As a result, South Ossetia is no longer under the control of Georgia. The flag used by the Republic of South Ossetia is a tricolor of white, red and yellow, with the white standing for spiritual life, the red for the military and the yellow for the well-being of the Ossetian people.

Population:	51,547
Capital:	Tskhinvali
Languages:	Ossetian, Russian
Currency:	Russian ruble

Temple of the Tooth, Kandy, Sri Lanka.

The Great Mosque of Damascus.

Sri Lanka

Sri Lanka lies south-east of India and until 1972 was known as Ceylon. The economy relies on tea, coconuts and rubber. Since independence, violence and civil war between the Sinhalese Buddhists and the Tamil Hindus has

brought continuous strife to the country. The flag was adopted three years after independence from the British in 1948. The lion on the banner represents the ancient Buddhist kingdom and the stripes are for the country's religious and ethnic minorities, green for the Muslims and orange for the Hindus.

Population:	20,675,000
Capital:	Colombo
Languages:	Sinhala, Tamil
Currency:	Sri Lankan rupee

Tea plantation, Sri Lanka.

Syria

Syria lies on the Mediterranean Sea and stretches inland as far as the Tigris river, with mountainous areas in the south and west. It lies at an important crossroads between Europe and Asia and this is reflected in its many historic and archeological sites. Syria officially became an independent country in

1946, but became part of the United Arab Republic, along with Egypt and Yemen, between 1958 and 1961. The flag dates from the year 1958 and displays the colors of the pan-Arab movement.

Population:	23,169,389
Capital:	Damascus
Languages:	Arabic
Currency:	Syrian pound

Sukhothai Historical Park, Thailand.

Tajikistan

(Tadzhikistan)

Tajikistan is mainly upland and lies between China, Kyrgyzstan, Uzbekistan and Afghanistan. Tajikistan became a unitary state in 1991 when it broke away from the U.S.S.R. It is mainly an Islamic country and remains very poor. The new flag dates from 1993 and shows a golden crown beneath seven stars. The colors of the flag derive from

Tajikistan's previous flag when it was part of the U.S.S.R.

Population:	8,354,000
Capital:	Dushanbe
Languages:	Tajik
Currency:	Somoni

Thailand

Thailand (known as Siam until 1939) is a tropical country situated in South-

East Asia. The country has been ruled by the Chakri dynasty since 1782, and is the only country in the region not to have been colonized by foreigners. During the 19th century, Thailand's flag featured a white elephant, which was a traditional symbol of the country, although this was removed in 1916 and the central blue stripe was added as a gesture of solidarity with the Allies in in First World War in 1917. The new colors of red, white, and blue were borrowed from the French flag.

Population:	65,104,000
Capital:	Bangkok
Languages:	Thai
Currency:	Baht

Lakeside village, Tajikistan.

Bangkok, Thailand.

Turkey

Turkey is a Muslim country, a small part of which is in Europe, while 97 per cent lies in Asia. It was once the centre of the Eastern Roman (Byzantine) Empire and later the core of the great Ottoman Empire which collapsed in the First World War. Despite attempts to modernize, Turkey remains a lower-middle-income economy. The flag displays the crescent moon and five-pointed star – two symbols of Islam which, together with the red background, are also typical of the flags used by the Ottoman rulers.

Population: 77,695,904
Capital: Ankara
Languages: Turkish
Currency: Turkish lira

The Galata Tower and Golden Horn, Istanbul, Turkey.

Turkmenistan

Turkmenistan is extremely arid with the vast Kara Kum Desert covering 90 per cent of the country. In 1991, it broke away from the former Soviet Union and has since formed close relationships with Muslim countries to the south. The flag was adopted in 1992. Turkmenistan is an important producer of carpets, so the design is particularly appropriate, with the five stars and the five elements of the carpet design standing for the five main peoples in the country.

Population: 4,751,120
Capital: Ashgabat (Ashkhabad)
Languages: Turkmen
Currency: Turkmen new manat

United Arab Emirates

The U.A.E. comprises seven federated emirates and was formed in 1971. Abu Dhabi, Ajman, Dubai, Fujairah, Sharjah and Umm al-Qaiwain first amalgamated, with Ras-al-Khaimah following in 1972. The U.A.E. lies on the Arabian Gulf and is hot and arid. The flag has all the pan-Arab colors signifying Arab unity and was formally adopted in 1971, although it actually dates to 1916, when it was used in a revolt against the Turks.

Population:	9,577,000
Capital:	Abu Dhabi
Languages:	Arabic
Currency:	U.A.E. dirham

Uzbekistan

Uzbekistan lies between Afghanistan and Kyrgyzstan. The country declared its independence from the former Soviet Union in 1990 and became a member of the Commonwealth of Independent States in 1991. In 1991, the old Soviet-style flag was replaced by the current one. The blue stands for Timur (Tamburlaine the Great), who once ruled Uzbekistan, white is for peace, green is for the country's natural vegetation and red is for

Abu Dhabi, United Arab Emirates.

Khiva, Uzbekistan.

vitality. The 12 stars represent the months of the Islamic calendar and the crescent moon is for the Islamic religion.

Population:	30,492,800
Capital:	Toshkent (Tashkent)
Languages:	Uzbek
Currency:	Som

Democratic Republic (South Yemen) have been unified as the Republic of Yemen, though southerners fought unsuccessfully for secession in 1994. Dating from unification, the flag is composed of the pan-Arab colors signifying Arab unity.

Vietnam

Vietnam lies in South-East Asia and is an amalgamation of the former states of North and South Vietnam. Once part of French Indochina, Vietnam broke away from French control in 1954, which resulted in a communist North Vietnam and non-communist South Vietnam. Despite American intervention, the whole of Vietnam became a communist state in 1975. The flag dates from 1955, originally adopted by North Vietnam, but became the flag for the whole country in 1975. It uses the same red field as the flag of China, with a single star symbolizing communism.

Population:	91,583,000
Capital:	Hanoi
Languages:	Vietnamese
Currency:	Dong

Yemen

Yemen is located at the southern end of the Arabian peninsula. Since 1990, the Yemen Arab Republic (North Yemen) and the Yemen People's

Population:	25,956,000
Capital:	San'aa
Languages:	Arabic
Currency:	Yemeni rial

Floating village in Halong Bay, Vietnam.

Haraz, Al-Hutaib, Yemen.

AFRICA

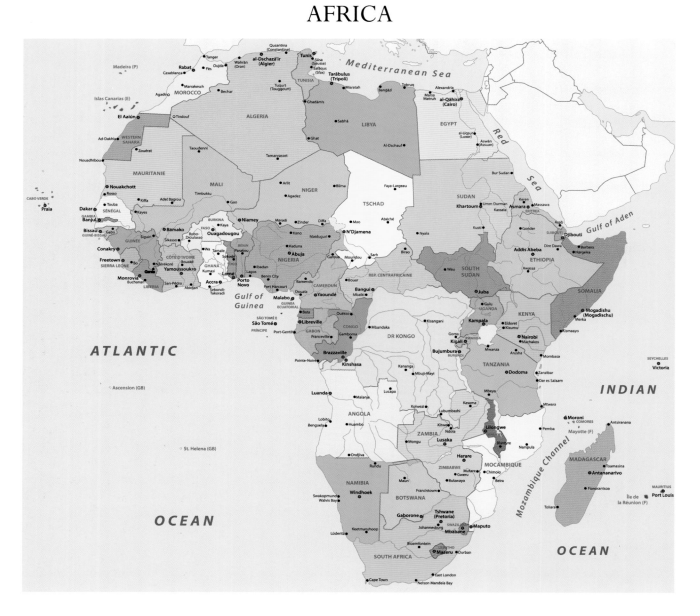

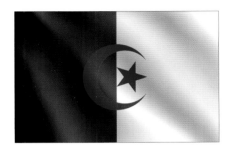

Algeria

Algeria is a large country with a great proportion of its area covered by the Sahara Desert. The harsh climate has caused most of its population to congregate along the Mediterranean coast. After a bitter struggle between nationalist guerillas and the French, Algeria achieved independence in 1962 and has since been ruled by the Front de Libération Nationale. The

Sahara Desert, Algeria.

flag of this political party is now the national flag, but it originally dates back to the 1920s when it symbolized resistance to the French. As always, the green stripe symbolizes Islam, the white purity, the Islamic crescent and star being a universal badge of Islam. The red is symbolic of bloodshed.

Population:	39,500,000
Capital:	Algiers
Languages:	Arabic
Currency:	Algerian dinar

Angola

Situated in south-west Africa, Angola has a widely varying climate and vegetation, from desert on the south coast to equatorial and montane conditions in the centre and north. After the arrival of the Portuguese in the late 15th century, Angola became a center of the slave trade; independence from Portugal was

Ruacana Falls, border of Angola and Namibia.

achieved in 1975. Potentially a wealthy country, Angola's development has been hampered by civil war. The five-pointed star, machete, and segment of a cog-wheel, are clearly inspired by the hammer and sickle used by the former U.S.S.R., representing the industrial and agricultural workers. It is said that the yellow represents the country's rich natural resources and the red and black stripes have been borrowed from other communist-liberated nations to mean 'Freedom or Death'.

Population:	24,383,301
Capital:	Luanda
Languages:	Portuguese
Currency:	Kwanza

Benin

A small, equatorial country in West Africa, Benin has a hot, wet climate with a belt of rain forest, the country becoming savanna in the north. Known as Dahomey until 1975, Benin has a history of Dutch, Portuguese and French colonial influence, and was much involved with the slave trade. Finally, the country gained independence in 1960, but it was not until 1991 that a multi-party democracy was established. The flag displays the red, yellow and green pan-African colors. Benin has another flag linked to its communist history; a plain green flag with a red communist star was used from 1975 until 1990, when Benin abandoned its socialist policies.

Population:	10,315,244
Capital:	Porto-Novo
Languages:	French
Currency:	Franc C.F.A.

Botswana

Situated in southern Africa, Botswana comprises swampland, desert and scrubland. Botswana was formerly known as Bechuanaland and was a British protectorate until 1966, when it became independent. The white, black, white stripe is intended to symbolize racial harmony with Europeans and Africans living in peaceful coexistence, the blue color representing water. A largely arid country, Botswana is dependent on a good yearly rainfall for its agriculture and its economy. Hence the national motto which is 'Let there be rain'.

Population:	2,056,000
Capital:	Gaborone
Languages:	English
Currency:	Pula

Betammaribe house, Benin.

Chobe river, Botswana.

Burkina Faso

Since independence from France in 1960, Burkina Faso, formerly Upper Volta, has adopted a new name and a new flag. Situated in West Africa, it is a landlocked country and is mostly lowland. Burkina Faso means 'The Land of the Honest People' or 'The Republic of Upright Men'. The flag colors of yellow, red and green are those of pan-Africa, seen in many African flags signifying unity and fellowship with other ex-colonial African nations. The large yellow star symbolizes the revolution. The flag was adopted in 1984, when the country's name was changed.

Population:	18,450,494
Capital:	Ouagadougou
Languages:	French
Currency:	Franc C.F.A.

Burundi

This small, landlocked African country next to Tanzania and supports a dense population. Burundi has a German and Belgian colonial history, finally gaining its independence in 1962 and establishing a republic in 1966. It was in 1966 that the flag we know today was adopted. The three green-edged red stars stand for Burundi's motto 'Unity, Work, Progress' and also for the three ethnic groups of the country. Conflict between the two major groups, the Hutu and Tutsi, has marred the country's development. Green represents hope for the future, red the struggle for independence and white the hope for peace.

Population:	9,823,827
Capital:	Bujumbura
Languages:	Kirundi, French
Currency:	Burundi franc

Mud-built mosque, Burkina Faso.

Lake Tanganyika, Burundi.

Burundi.

Cameroon

Cameroon is located in west-central Africa and its colonial history accounts for its French, British and German influences. It was ruled as a German protectorate until 1884, but ended up being divided between the French and the British. Independence

Cameroon.

Bay of Faja D'Agua, Brava, Cape Verde.

was achieved in 1960–1961 when part of the British territory joined Nigeria. The federation of British and French states became a military state in 1972. A republic was created in 1984. The green, red and yellow are the pan-African colors. The design of the flag is based on the French tricolor, the yellow star representing liberty.

Population:	21,143,237
Capital:	Yaoundé
Languages:	French, English
Currency:	Franc C.F.A.

Cape Verde

The Cape Verde islands lie off the coast of Senegal and are volcanic and mountainous. The country belonged to Portugal from 1462–1974, finally becaming independent in 1975. The islands are poor, not over-endowed with good natural resources, and are therefore dependent on foreign aid, which has led to a high rate of emigration. Cape Verde has a relatively new flag, established in September 1992 to signify the end of rule by PAIGC, the 'Partido Africano da Independencia da Guine e Cabo Verde', and the movement towards democracy.

Population:	518,467
Capital:	Praia
Languages:	Portuguese
Currency:	Cape Verde escudo

Central African Republic

Formerly known as Ubangi-Shari, the Central African Republic was once a province of French Equatorial Africa. Its rivers flow south into the Zaire basin and north to Lake Chad, creating a watershed area between the Zaire and Chad basins. It became independent in 1960. Since then, the Central African Republic has experienced difficulty, having had one of Africa's most repressive regimes between 1966 and 1979. Multiparty elections took place in 1993. The flag was adopted in 1958, two years prior to independence, the green, yellow and red signifying pan-African unity. It also echoes the tricolor of France, the country's former ruler.

Population:	4,803,000
Capital:	Bangui
Languages:	French
Currency:	Franc C.F.A.

Elephants in a jungle clearing, Central African Republic.

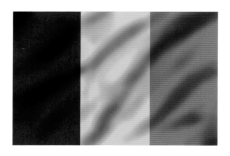

Chad

A large state south of Libya, Chad is Africa's largest landlocked country and occupies part of the Sahara Desert. Chad achieved independence from France in 1960, then suffered continuous civil war between ethnic groups in the north and south. The Aouzou Strip, in northern Chad, has also been occupied by Libya since 1973, but in 1994 the International Court of Justice ruled in favor of Chad, although Libyan troops have remained there despite the ruling. The flag is a combination of the French tricolor and the colors of pan-African unity. Blue represents the tropical sky, the streams and hope, yellow the desert and the sun, and red the sacrifice for freedom and bloodshed.

Population: 13,606,000
Capital: N'Djamena
Languages: French, Arabic
Currency: Franc C.F.A.

Comoros

The Comoros Islands lie off the East African coast north-west of Madagascar. The islands became independent following a referendum in 1974 when ties were finally broken with France, although the people of one island, Mayotte, voted to remain French. The islands constitute one of the world's poorest countries. The crescent in the green background represents the Muslim faith and the four stars the four islands, as do the horizontal stripes.

Population: 763,952
Capital: Moroni
Languages: Swahili, French
Currency: Comorian franc

Sahara Desert, Chad.

Comoros.

Congo, Democratic Republic of the

Formerly Zäire, the Democratic Republic of the Congo extends over a large area, much of which lies in the drainage basin on the River Congo. Dense rainforests grow in the north, with savanna to the south. Once a possession of the Belgian crown in 1885, it was a colony from 1908 until it gained independence in 1960. The current flag dates to 2006, with the light blue field symbolizing hope, the red the blood shed for freedom, the narrow gold stripes prosperity, and the star unity.

Population:	71,246,000
Capital:	Kinshasa
Languages:	French
Currency:	Congolese franc

Congo, Republic of the

The Republic of the Congo is an equatorial country, with a climate that is extremely hot with all-year-round rainfall. Congo was part of French Equatorial Africa until it gained independence in 1960. It declared itself communist in 1970 and remained so until 1990 when Marxism was abandoned. Elections were held in 1992 and a multi-party republic was created. The new flag was adopted in 1990 and bears the colors of pan-African unity.

Population:	4,671,000
Capital:	Brazzaville
Languages:	French
Currency:	CFA franc

The view towards the Republic of the Congo across the River Nile.

Côte d'Ivoire

Lying in West Africa, on the Gulf of Guinea, the Ivory Coast has been officially known by its French name, the Côte d'Ivoire, since 1986. It has a tropical climate with substantial rain forests in the southern region. French influence dates back to the late-15th century when the trade in slaves and ivory became important. The country was controlled by the French from 1893 until 1960, when it became independent. The flag is a combination of the French tricolor and pan-African colors signifying African unity. The orange stripe is for the northern savanna, the white for peace and unity and the green for the rain forests in the south.

Population:	22,671,331
Capital:	Yamoussoukro
Languages:	French
Currency:	Franc C.F.A.

Djibouti

A small country in eastern Africa, Djibouti faces the Gulf of Aden and lies in a hot, arid unproductive plain. The country is strategically placed, due to the railway link with Addis Ababa, and is Ethiopia's main artery for overseas trade. Previously French territory, Djibouti gained independence in 1977, which was when the flag was adopted. The two main ethnic groups are the Afars and the Issas, the green representing the Afars and the blue the Issas. The white is for peace, with the red, five-pointed star symbolizing unity and independence.

Population:	900,000
Capital:	Djibouti
Languages:	Arabic, French
Currency:	Djibouti franc

Lac Assal, Djibouti.

Cairo, Egypt.

Egypt

Egypt is a large country with a third of its area covered by desert. The fertile Nile Valley and its delta support 96 per cent of the population. Egypt was part of the Ottoman Empire from 1517, although British influence became important later on. The country was a British protectorate from 1914 to 1922 when it became partially independent. The present republic was established in 1953 after the corrupt régime of King Farouk had been toppled by a military coup. Since 1958, the flag of Egypt has been a red, white and black tricolor, although the emblem in the centre has varied from time to time. The current design bears a golden eagle symbolizing Saladin, the hero who led the Arabs in the 12th century.

Population:	88,426,800
Capital:	Cairo
Languages:	Arabic
Currency:	Egyptian pound

Pyramids at Giza, Egypt.

After a long struggle, Eritrea declared independence on 24 May 1993 and broke away from Ethiopia, the new flag being a variation on that of the Eritrean People's Liberation Front. The flag features an olive wreath, which was taken from an older flag used between 1952 and 1959.

Equatorial Guinea

Equatorial Guinea is located in West Africa and comprises a mainland area, called Mbini, and five mountainous and volcanic islands. The capital, Malabo, is situated on the largest of the islands, which is called Bioko. This was one of the last African countries to achieve independence, which took place in 1968. The flag was altered during the dictatorship of Francisco Nguema (1972–1979) but has now been restored to its 1968 form. The emblem depicts a silk cotton tree with six stars representing the mainland and islands. Green symbolizes the country's natural resources, the blue the sea, the red the struggle for freedom, and the white peace.

Population:	1,430,000
Capital:	Malabo
Languages:	Spanish,
Currency:	Franc C.F.A.

Eritrea

Eritrea was a colony of Italy until 1941, administered thereafter by the British military until 1952, when it became an autonomous region within the Federation of Ethiopia and Eritrea.

Population:	6,738,000
Capital:	Asmera
Languages:	Tigrinya
Currency:	Eritrea nakfa

Asmera, capital of Eritrea.

Ethiopia

Ethiopia is a mountainous country featuring part of the Great Rift Valley. The Blue Nile and its tributaries originate here, and Ethiopia suffers from periods of severe drought. Until 1936 it was the only African country not conquered by the Europeans, which ended when Italy invaded and ruled until 1941. After British troops forced the Italians out, Emperor Haile Selassie ruled the country until 1974 when he was deposed by a military coup. Ethiopia was declared a socialist state and President Mengistu took control in 1977 with a period of 'Red Terror'. The military regime collapsed in 1991, and Ethiopia is now working towards a democratic federal system of government. The Ethiopian flag has become the basis for many other African flags signifying pan-Africanism, and first appeared in 1897. The seal of Solomon was added in 1996 to symbolize the diversity of the country.

Population:	90,076,012
Capital:	Addis Ababa
Languages:	Amharic
Currency:	Birr

Gabon

Gabon lies on the equator in West Africa, having taken its name from Gabão, a 16th-century Portuguese explorer. The climate is humid and hot with a high rainfall, and the country has rich forest and mineral resources. Gabon was a French colony from the 1880s until independence in 1960, when the flag was first adopted. The yellow stripe representing the sun may also symbolize the equator, with the green stripe standing for the forest and the blue for the sea.

Population:	1,751,000
Capital:	Libreville
Languages:	French
Currency:	Franc C.F.A.

Farmland, Ethiopia.

Gambia

The Republic of the Gambia lies in the far west of Africa, it being a long, narrow country following the course of the River Gambia. It is almost completely surrounded by Senegal. Once part of the great Mali empire, Gambia became involved in the slave trade after the arrival of the Portuguese in the 15th century, who were supplanted by the British who made this a colony in 1843. Independence came in 1965 and with it the flag, as we see it today, was adopted. The blue stripes symbolize the River Gambia, the red the sun, and the green the land.

Population:	1,882,450
Capital:	Banjul
Languages:	English
Currency:	Dalasi

Wassu stone circles in Gambia.

Ghana

The West African country of Ghana faces the Gulf of Guinea, with its southern coast on the Atlantic Ocean. In the 17th century, the area became a centre of the slave trade which lasted until the 1860s. Formerly known as the Gold Coast, the country took the name Ghana in 1957, when it became independent. The flag, adopted in 1957, is red, yellow and green, pan-African colors which signify African unity and which were first used by Ethiopia, the oldest independent nation in Africa. The black star is a symbol of African freedom.

Population:	27,043,093
Capital:	Accra
Languages:	English
Currency:	Cedi

A fishing village in Axim, northern Ghana.

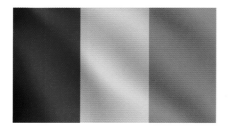

Guinea

Guinea is a country of varied landscapes facing the Atlantic Ocean in West Africa. The flag was first introduced shortly after independence from France in 1958. It is based on the French tricolor, but uses the pan-African colors. The colors symbolize the three words of the national motto, 'Travail, Justice, Solidarity', the red being for work, the yellow for justice and the green for solidarity.

Population: 10,628,972
Capital: Conakry
Languages: French
Currency: Guinea franc

Guinea-Bissau

Lying between Guinea and Senegal in West Africa, Guinea-Bissau is a small, low-lying, tropical country with a swampy coastal area. It has many offshore islands. Guinea-Bissau was once known as Portuguese Guinea and was ruled by the Portuguese for 500 years until independence in 1973. The flag has adopted the pan-African colors, the five-pointed star indicating African freedom. The flag is very similar to that which was adopted by Cape Verde, but now superseded, both flags having derived from that of the Partido Africano da Independence da Guine e Cabo Verde (PAIGC).

Population: 1,788,000
Capital: Bissau
Languages: Portuguese
Currency: Franc C.F.A.

Kenya

An equatorial country, Kenya lies in East Africa on the Indian Ocean. The climate is tropical. Kenya has been a centre for trading for thousands of years, and the area has been influenced by Arabs, Portuguese and the British who took over in 1895. Kenya became independent in 1963 when the flag was adopted. It is based on that of the Kenya African National Union, the organization which led the movement towards independence from the British. The central image is a Masai warrior's shield with crossed spears.

Population: 46,749,000
Capital: Nairobi
Languages: English, Swahili
Currency: Kenya shilling

Mount Kilimanjaro, Amboseli National Park, Kenya.

Lesotho

The Kingdom of Lesotho is a small, mountainous country with the River Orange running through it. The climate makes agriculture difficult, although most of the population survives through subsistence farming, with many seeking work in neighboring South Africa. The country was a British protectorate from 1868 until 1966, when it became independent. In 1986 the leader of the Lesotho National Party was deposed and new military rulers took over, issuing a new flag. In 2006, however, the flag was changed again, but the combination of colors remained the same, with white for peace, blue for rain and green for prosperity. The symbol in the centre of the flag is a black Basotho hat.

Population:	2,120,000
Capital:	Maseru
Languages:	Sotho, English
Currency:	Loti

Liberia

Situated in West Africa, Liberia is sparsely populated and covered mainly by tropical rain forest. Liberia, as the name suggests, was founded as an American colony for freed black slaves in 1821–1822, becoming the first new independent state of modem Africa when independence was declared in 1847. The flag derives from the American Stars and Stripes, that represent the 11 men who signed the Declaration of Independence. The single white star symbolizes the 'shining light in the dark continent'.

Population:	4,503,000
Capital:	Monrovia
Languages:	English
Currency:	Liberian dollar

Basotho huts, Lesotho.

Libya

Libya is a large country bordering the Mediterranean Sea. It has a harsh, arid climate and much of the country is desert, although the coastal area is more fertile. Libya was controlled by the Italians from 1912 until they were defeated in the Second World War. In 1969, the monarchy of Libya was overthrown in a coup led by Colonel Gaddafi. Following the death of the dicator in 2011, the former solid green flag was replaced, the new one being identical to the flag used between 1951 and 1969. The colors represent the three major regions of the country, with red for Fezzan, black for Cyrenaica and green for Tripolitania. The crescent and star represent Islam.

Population:	6,317,000
Capital:	Tripoli
Languages:	Arabic
Currency:	Libyan dinar

Leptis Magna, Tripoli, Libya.

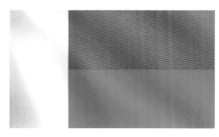

Madagascar

Madagascar is a large island located off the east coast of Africa, and has a varied climate, due to its size, ranging from arid to hot and wet. Despite its proximity to Africa, Madagascar is largely populated by Malayo-Polynesians. Once occupied by the

Ring-tailed lemur, Madagascar.

French, the island still retains much of its French influence. Since gaining independence in 1958, the country continued its links with France until it became a socialist dictatorship in 1975, and it was only in 1991 that this regime was defeated. Presidential elections took place in 1992/1993, but the country remains very poor. The white, red and green of Madagascar's flag had its origins in the colors of many South-East Asian countries, and was adopted in 1958 when the country first became independent.

Population:	21,842,167
Capital:	Antananarivo
Languages:	Malagasy, French
Currency:	Malagasy ariary

Malawi

Malawi is a small country by African standards. A British protectorate under the name Nyasaland from 1891, the country gained independence from Britain in 1964 and the Malawi Congress Party, led by Dr. Hastings Kamuzu Banda, took control, declaring himself president for life in 1971. Under his control, Malawi saw brief periods of growth, but the country remains predominantly very poor. Banda was defeated in elections in 1994 and was replaced as president by Bakili Muluzi. The flag dates back to 1953 when the Malawi Congress Party was first established. The rising sun symbolizes the dawning of a new era and the colors are those of the Black Liberation Movement.

Population:	16,310,431
Capital:	Lilongwe
Languages:	English
Currency:	Malawian kwacha

Mali

Mali is a poor, landlocked country in West Africa, much of which lies within the Sahara Desert, making the population extremely reliant upon the Senegal and Niger rivers for their survival. Mali became independent from France in 1960 but soon became dominated by the repressive rule of Moussa Traoré. Mali freed itself of this régime in 1991, after a revolution. The flag dates back to 1959 and is made up of the pan-African colors symbolizing African unity. The center of the flag originally featured a stylized figure, but this was dropped in 1961.

Population:	16,259,000
Capital:	Bamako
Languages:	French
Currency:	Franc C.F.A.

Lake Malawi, Malawi.

Great Mosque of Djenné, Mali.

Mauritania

Much of Mauritania is covered by the Sahara Desert, with agriculture based mainly along the Senegal river. In recent years, persistent drought devastated the herds of the nomadic population. Originally part of French West Africa, Mauritania became fully independent in 1960, the flag having been introduced in 1959, a year prior to independence. The green background to the flag, with the yellow crescent and star, are typical devices used by Islamic countries.

Population:	3,631,775
Capital:	Nouakchott
Languages:	Arabic
Currency:	Ouguiya

Mauritius

Mauritius lies off the coast of East Africa and consists of the main island with many reefs and smaller islets in the vicinity. Mauritius was settled by the Dutch in 1639, followed by the French and then the British. It finally became independent in 1968 when the flag was first adopted, the colors of which – red, blue, yellow and green – being those of the coat of arms dating back to 1906. Red symbolizes for the struggle for independence, blue for the Indian Ocean, yellow for the bright future and sunlight, and green for the vegetation and agriculture of the country.

Population:	1,261,208
Capital:	Port Louis
Languages:	English
Currency:	Mauritius rupee

Tropical lagoon, Mauritius.

Port Louis, Mauritius.

Morocco

Morocco occupies the north-western corner of Africa. Peasant agriculture and nomadic pastoralism make up much of the economy, although in recent years, tourism has become increasingly more important. Morocco has been ruled by the Sharifian dynasty since the 16th century, though Spain laid claim to coastal settlements which became enclaves in the 19th century. In 1912, Morocco became a French protectorate with areas controlled by Spain until 1956, when it gained independence. Its flag was originally plain red, like many other Arab countries, and dates back to the 16th century. The green star, 'Solomon's Seal', was added in 1915, and is a religious emblem.

Population:	33,848,242
Capital:	Rabat
Languages:	Arabic
Currency:	Moroccan dirham

The fortified city of Aït Benhaddou, Morocco.

Fez, Morocco.

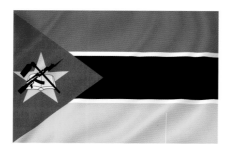

Mozambique

Mozambique lies in south-east Africa and has a tropical climate. After breaking ties with Portugal in 1975 the country was plunged into civil war, accompanied by a series of droughts and floods. As a consequence, the country remains poor. The colors of the flag derive from those used by the Frelimo party, which led the struggle for independence from the Portuguese. Frelimo won a majority of seats in multi-party elections held in 1994, with the former guerrilla group, Renamo, coming second. The current flag was adopted in 1983 and is more closely based on the original Frelimo flag, with the green representing the land, the black stripe Africa and the yellow stripe mineral wealth. It includes the image of an AK-47 with a bayonet attached to the barrel, and is the only national flag in the world to feature such a modern rifle, the other devices being Marxist symbols. Marxism was relinquished in 1989 and free multi-party elections were held in 1995.

Population:	25,727,911
Capital:	Maputo
Languages:	Portuguese
Currency:	Metical

Sodwana Bay Nature Reserve, Mozambique.

Namibia

Namibia occupies a large area in the south-west comer of Africa. With rich natural resources, the country has a varied landscape, ranging from desert coastline to mountain regions. Apart from a minor British influence, the majority of the country was under German control as a protectorate from 1884. During the First World War, Namibia was removed from German control and placed in the hands of the Union of South Africa at the request of the Allies. It was not until 1990 that the country achieved full independence. The flag is relatively new, dating from 1990, and is derived from that of SWAPO (South-West Africa People's Organization), which led the struggle against the South African occupation of Namibia. The green, blue and the golden sun represent the natural resources of the country, with the red and white symbolizing the people.

Population:	2,280,700
Capital:	Windhoek
Languages:	English
Currency:	Namibian dollar

The sand dunes of Sossusvlei in the Namib Desert, Namibia.

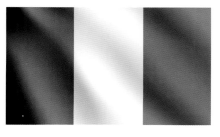

Niger

Niger is a large, landlocked African country. With desert to the north and a substantial mountainous area, only a small proportion of the area where the River Niger flows is cultivable. Like Nigeria, Niger is named after the river which flows through it. It was formerly a French colony but achieved independence in 1960. The flag dates back to 1959. The orange stripe represents the desert and the white the unity and purity of the people. The orange disc symbolizes the sun and the green stripe the Niger Valley.

Population:	19,268,000
Capital:	Niamey
Languages:	French
Currency:	Franc C.F.A.

Nigeria

Situated on the West African coast, Nigeria is a large, highly-populated country. With a terrain ranging from tropical rain forest, savanna and mountains to mangrove swamps and sandy beaches, the terrain is extremely varied. Nigeria was a British colony between 1914 and 1960. From 1967 to 1970, the country experienced a bitter civil war when the Ibo people of Biafra, in Nigeria's eastern region, declared independence but were defeated. The flag was adopted in 1960, the design having been a winning entry in a competition. The green represents the country's agriculture and forests and the white is for peace.

Population:	183,523,000
Capital:	Abuja
Languages:	English
Currency:	Naira

Lagos, Nigeria.

A remote school in Idanre, Ondo State, Nigeria.

Rwanda

Rwanda is a small, landlocked country with a population that is dense and very poor, relying mainly on agriculture. Rwanda was part of German East Africa, but during the First World War was occupied by Belgium and became the UN Trust Territory of Ruanda-Urundi, finally achieving independence in 1962. The southern part of Ruanda-Urundi is now Burundi. Since independence, fierce conflict between the country's two main ethnic groups, the Hutu and the Tutsi, has seriously damaged the country's development. The flag is dissected by three bands, with the blue for hope and the promise of peace, the sun for enlightenment, the yellow for the need for reconstruction and the green for prosperity.

Population:	10,996,891
Capital:	Kigali
Languages:	Kinyarwanda, English
Currency:	Rwanda franc

Young gorilla in Volcanoes National Park, Rwanda.

São Tomé and Príncipe

The state consists of two small islands in the Gulf of Guinea, these being mountainous, volcanic and heavily forested. The islands became a Portuguese colony in 1522 and gained

Sao Sebastiao Fort, São Tomé & Príncipe.

their independence in 1975. Dating from independence, the flag has the traditional pan-African colors signifying African unity, and is based on that used by the national liberation movement prior to independence. The two black stars represent the two islands.

Population:	187,356
Capital:	São Tomé
Languages:	Portuguese
Currency:	Dobra

Praia Piscina, São Tomé & Príncipe.

Senegal

Senegal is situated in the far west of Africa, with Dakar, with its industrial center, being by far the largest city. Senegal was France's oldest colony and became the administrative centre for French West Africa. A year prior to independence in 1960, it joined the Federation of Mali and the two countries adopted a joint flag. After independence, however, the two countries went their separate ways and an attempted federation with Gambia in 1981–1989 also failed. Mali kept the old flag, but that of Senegal is very similar, with a green five-pointed star symbolizing the Muslim faith. The colors of the flag were originally chosen to show solidarity with Ghana.

Population:	13,508,715
Capital:	Dakar
Languages:	French
Currency:	Franc C.F.A.

Mosque of Divinity, Dakar, Senegal.

Seychelles

The Seychelles consist of over 100 islands in the Indian Ocean, many of which are uninhabited. The country was a French colony from 1756 and British from 1814. On independence in 1976, the Seychelles adopted a flag that combined the colors of the two leading political parties, the Democrats and the Seychelles People's United Party. One year later, however, the People's United Party seized power. The Seychelles became a multi-party democracy in 1993 when the current flag was adopted. The five colour bands, radiating from the lower right, represent the colors of the two main political parties, the green and white representing the ruling Seychelles People's party, and the blue and yellow the Democrats. The red is common to both parties.

Population:	89,949
Capital:	Victoria
Languages:	Creole, English, French
Currency:	Seychelles rupee

La Digue, Seychelles.

Sierra Leone

Located on the coast of West Africa, Sierra Leone has a hot, tropical, climate, with swampy areas near the coast and high mountains and plateaux in the interior. Sierra Leone means 'The Lion Mountains' and, like Liberia, was intended as a home for freed slaves when it was founded by British philanthropists in 1787, the capital being named Freetown. A British colony from 1808, Sierra Leone became independent in 1961 when the new flag was introduced, the colors of which derive from the country's coat of arms. The green stands for agriculture, the white for unity and peace and the blue for the Atlantic Ocean.

Population:	6,319,000
Capital:	Freetown
Languages:	English
Currency:	Leone

Berbera, Somalia.

Somalia

The Somali Republic, or Somalia as it is also known, is situated partly on the Gulf of Aden and also on the Indian Ocean. The country was ruled by both the British and Italians, with independence arriving in 1960 when the two European colonies united. The flag takes its colors from that of the United Nations; the five-pointed star represents the five main regions where the Somalis live, those being northern Kenya, Ethiopia, French Somaliland (now Djibouti), British Somaliland and Italian Somaliland. The star itself represents African freedom.

Population:	11,123,000
Capital:	Mogadishu
Languages:	Somali, Arabic
Currency:	Somali shilling

Freetown, Sierra Leone.

The Cape Town waterfront and Table Mountain, South Africa.

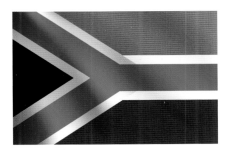

South Africa

South Africa came into existence as a result of a union in 1910 between Boer (Afrikaner) and British territories following two and a half centuries of European settlement and conquest. Domination of the black population began early, resulting in the introduction of apartheid in 1948, when discrimination and racial segregation were stringently enforced. In 1989, however, reforms began with multiracial elections being held in 1994 and a new black president, Nelson Mandela, was elected. At this time, the new flag was introduced. It combines the colors of the European peoples (red, white and blue) with those of the African National Congress (black, yellow and green).

Population: 54,002,000
Capital: Pretoria, Cape Town, Bloemfontein
Languages: Afrikaans, English, African languages
Currency: Rand

South Sudan

South Sudan, officially the Republic of South Sudan, is a landlocked country in north-eastern Africa. The flag was adopted following the signing of the Comprehensive Peace Agreement that ended the Sudanese Civil War in 2011, and had previously been used as that of the Sudan People's Liberation movement. It bears striking similarities to the flag of Sudan, the black being for African skin, the red for bloodshed, the green for the country's natural resources, the white for peace, the blue for the River Nile and the yellow for unity.

Population: 11,892,934
Capital: Juba
Languages: English
Currency: South Sudanese pound

Traditional village, South Sudan.

Sudan

Sudan is the largest country in Africa and consists mainly of great plains. It includes part of the Nile basin and Sahara Desert, and much of the country is uninhabited, with the majority of the population living by the waters of the White and Blue Niles. In 1956, Sudan became independent of Britain and Egypt, which had ruled it since 1889. Since independence, however, the country has been plunged into civil wars between the Muslims in the north and the non-Muslim population in the south. The flag, the design of which was a winning entry in a competition, was adopted in 1969, and features the pan-Arab colors with an Islamic green triangle.

Population: 38,435,252
Capital: Khartoum
Languages: Arabic
Currency: Sudanese pound

The Meroë Pyramids, Sudan.

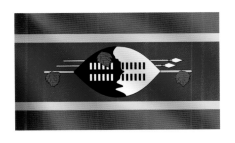

Swaziland

Swaziland is a small, landlocked country in southern Africa with a varied landscape. In 1902, Britain took control of the country, which remained British until 1968 when it achieved independence. Swaziland has a distinctive flag which was adopted on independence. It is based on one designed for the Swazi Pioneer Corps in 1941 and is therefore related to flags used in the British Army. The emblems, however, are pure Swazi, and show the weapons of a warrior, i.e., ox-hide shield, two assegai (spears) and a fighting stick.

Population:	1,119,375
Capital:	Mbabane
Languages:	English, Swazi
Currency:	Lilangeni

Tanzania

Tanzania lies across the high plateau of East Africa where the extinct volcano of Kilimanjaro, the highest mountain in Africa, is to be found. The country of Tanzania dates from 1964 when Tanganyika and Zanzibar united, and it has adopted the colors of these former countries. Green is representative of agricultural resources, green of mineral wealth, while black is for the people, with blue representing water and Zanzibar.

Population:	47,421,876
Capital:	Dodoma
Languages:	English, Swahili
Currency:	Tanzanian shilling

Swaziland landscape.

Mount Kilimanjaro, Tanzania.

Forte El Ribat, Monastir, Tunisia.

Togo

Togo lies in West Africa and stretches north from the Gulf of Guinea. The first Europeans to reach Togo were the Portuguese, in the late 15th century, and it later became a frontrunner in the slave trade. In 1884, the country was colonized by Germany, but the territory was occupied by the French and the British after the First World War. Later, the British sector became part of Ghana and the French became independent in 1960 as Togo. Based on the stars and stripes, Togo's flag bears the pan-African colors representing African unity. Green represents agriculture, red bloodshed, yellow the mineral resources, while white is for purity. The five stripes symbolize the five administrative areas of Togo.

Population:	7,171,000
Capital:	Lomé
Languages:	French
Currency:	Franc C.F.A.

Tunisia

Tunisia is the smallest country in North Africa and is located on the Mediterranean Coast. It has a long and varied history, with strong influences from the Arabs, Turks, Romans, and later from the French, who ruled Tunisia from 1881 to 1956. The flag features the five-pointed star and the crescent moon, both of which symbolize Islam. Dating from 1835, the flag is based on the Turkish flag, but was not officially adopted until 1923.

Population:	10,982,754
Capital:	Tunis
Languages:	Arabic
Currency:	Tunisian dinar

View of the medina and Castle Kasbah, Sousse, Tunisia.

Lake Bunyonyi, Uganda.

Uganda

The Republic of Uganda is a landlocked country in East Africa and contains part of Lake Victoria. In the south, Uganda has rain forests, while the north is somewhat drier, with savanna and grassland. The British took over the country in 1894 and ruled it until independence in 1962, following which came a succession of civil wars, violence and massacres. The flag was adopted in 1962 and is based on the colors of the Uganda People's Congress, which was in power at the time of independence. Black represents the people, yellow the sun and red is for brotherhood. In the centre of the flag is a red-crested crane, which is the country's emblem.

Population: 34,856,813
Capital: Kampala
Languages: Swahili, English
Currency: Shilling

The Kazinga Channel, Queen Elizabeth National Park, Uganda.

Western Sahara

Western Sahara is a disputed territory in the Maghreb region of North Africa, bordered by Morocco to the north, Algeria to the north-east, Mauritania to the east and south and the Atlantic Ocean to the west. Following a guerilla war in 1991, contesting

Coastal landscape, Western Sahara.

Moroccan sovereignty, the UN brokered a ceasefire, but the territory still remains in dispute. The flag is a combination of the pan-Arab colors of black, green, white and red and includes the Islamic symbols of the star and crescent. Red represents bloodshed, and the struggle for independence, black the period of colonization, white is for peace and green for progress.

Population: 510,713
Capital: Laayoune
Languages: Arabic
Currency: Moroccan dirham

193

Zambia

For the first half of the 20th century, when it was controlled first by the British South Africa Company and then became a colony, Zambia was known as Northern Rhodesia. It contains a large area of high plateaux and is situated in south-central Africa. The Victoria Falls lie on its border with Zimbabwe. The flag dates from independence from Britain in 1964, when the name Zambia was adopted. The orange stands for the mineral resources of the country, the black for the people and the red for the struggles of the country. The soaring eagle represents freedom and independence and the green background is for agriculture and forestry.

Population:	15,473,905
Capital:	Lusaka
Languages:	English
Currency:	Zambian kwacha

Zimbabwe

Zimbabwe is located in south-central Africa and is covered by vast areas of grassland. Britain colonized Zimbabwe in 1894, naming it Southern Rhodesia. In 1965 the conservative white minority government unilaterally declared independence as Rhodesia. The state endured international isolation and a 15-year guerrilla war with black nationalist forces; this culminated in a peace agreement that established universal enfranchisement and sovereignty in April 1980. This is when the flag was adopted, the colors of the flag having been taken from those of the ruling Patriotic Front.

Population:	13,061,239
Capital:	Harare
Languages:	English
Currency:	Zimbabwe dollar

Zambezi river, Zambia.

Victoria Falls, Zimbabwe.

CHAPTER SIX

AUSTRALASIA & THE PACIFIC

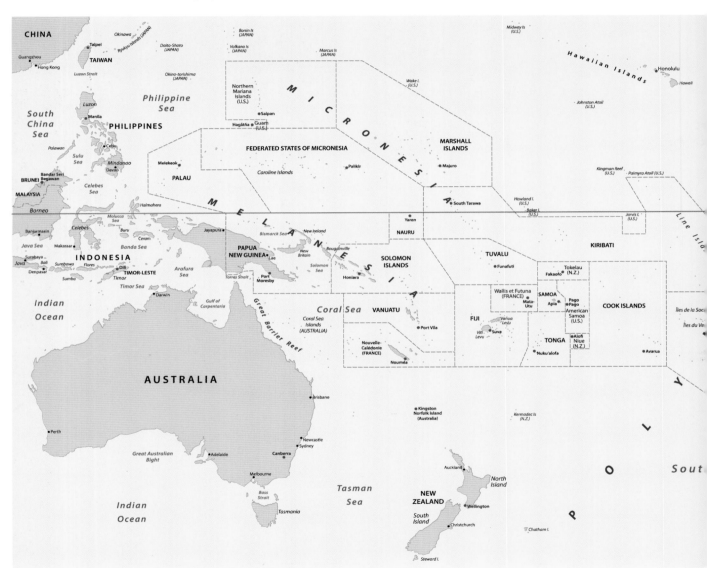

CHINA

Guangzhou
Hong Kong

TAIWAN
Taipei

Okinawa
Ryukyu Islands (JAPAN)

Daito-Shoto
(JAPAN)

Okino-torishima
(JAPAN)

Bonin Is
(JAPAN)

Volkano Is
(JAPAN)

Marcus Is
(JAPAN)

Midway Is
(U.S.)

Hawaiian Islands
Honolulu
Hawaii

Luzon Strait

Philippine
Sea

South
China
Sea

Luzon

Manila

PHILIPPINES

Palawan

Sulu
Sea

Cebu

Mindanao

Davao

Northern
Mariana
Islands
(U.S.)

Salpan

Hagåtña
Guam
(U.S.)

Wake I.
(U.S.)

Johnston Atoll
(U.S.)

MICRONESIA

MARSHALL
ISLANDS

Majuro

Kingman Reef
(U.S.)

Palmyra Atoll (U.S.)

BRUNEI
Bandar Seri
Begawan

MALAYSIA

Melekeok

PALAU

FEDERATED STATES OF MICRONESIA

Palikir

Caroline Islands

Celebes
Sea

Borneo

Halmahera

MELANESIA

South Tarawa

Howland I.
(U.S.)

Baker I.
(U.S.)

Jarvis I.
(U.S.)

Line Isla

Banjarmasin

Celebes

Molucca
Sea

Buru

Ceram

Java Sea

Makassar

Banda Sea

Jayapura

Bismarck Sea

New Ireland

Yaren

NAURU

KIRIBATI

Surabaya
Bali

INDONESIA

Java

Denpasar

Sumbawa

Flores

Sumba

Timor

Dili

TIMOR-LESTE

Arafura
Sea

Timor Sea

Torres Strait

PAPUA
NEW GUINEA

Lae

New
Britain

Bougainville

Solomon
Sea

Honiara

SOLOMON
ISLANDS

TUVALU

Funafuti

Tokelau
(N.Z.)

Fakaofo

Indian
Ocean

Darwin

Gulf of
Carpentaria

Port
Moresby

Coral Sea
Islands
(AUSTRALIA)

Coral Sea

VANUATU

Port Vila

Wallis et Futuna
(FRANCE)

Mata-
Utu

FIJI

Vanua
Levu

Viti
Levu

Suva

SAMOA

Apia

Pago
Pago

American
Samoa
(U.S.)

COOK ISLANDS

Îles de la Soci

Îles du Ve

Great Barrier Reef

Nouvelle-
Calédonie
(FRANCE)

Nouméa

TONGA

Nuku'alofa

Alofi
Niue
(N.Z.)

Avarua

AUSTRALIA

Brisbane

Perth

Great Australian
Bight

Adelaide

Canberra

Newcastle
Sydney

Melbourne

Kingston
Norfolk Island
(Australia)

Kermadec Is
(N.Z.)

P

O

L

Y

Sout

Bass
Strait

Tasman
Sea

Auckland

North
Island

NEW
ZEALAND

South
Island

Wellington

Christchurch

Indian
Ocean

Tasmania

Chatham I.

Steward I.

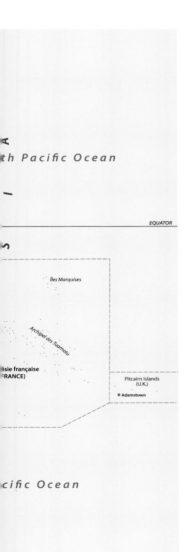

The Sydney Opera, Australia.

Australia

A vast country, largely made up of desert and semi-desert, with the majority of the population living in coastal areas, Australia has a fascinating geography. Its flag was adopted in 1901, the result of a winning entry in a competition. Clearly it shows Australia's links with Britain, with the flag featuring the blue ensign. The star formation represents the constellation of the Southern Cross, an emblem that has been used to symbolize the continent since its very early days. The larger seven-pointed Commonwealth Star represents the six states and the

Gold Coast, Queensland.

territories. A separate flag for Australia's aboriginal people was introduced in 1972.

Population: 23,826,300
Capital: Canberra
Languages: English
Currency: Australian dollar

Brisbane.

The south-eastern side of Uluru, Northern Territory, Australia.

The Yasawa Islands, Fiji.

Fiji

Fiji comprises more than 300 Melanesian islands which were discovered by the Dutch explorer, Abel Tasman, in 1643. Fiji became a British Crown Colony in 1874 and it took nearly 100 years for the country to gain its independence in 1970. The flag is clearly based on the blue ensign, but with a paler background than the traditional flag. The coat of arms shows a British lion, sugar cane, a coconut palm, a dove of peace and bananas.

Population:	859,178
Capital:	Suva
Languages:	English
Currency:	Fiji dollar

Kiribati

Situated in the Pacific Ocean, Kiribati is made up of groups of coral atolls. The islands are very poor and over-crowded and thus dependent on foreign aid. Previously known as the Gilbert Islands, the name was changed to Kiribati on independence from Britain in 1979. The flag shows the arms granted to the Gilbert & Ellice Islands in 1937, which consists of a yellow frigate bird above a sun rising over the Pacific Ocean.

Population:	106,461
Capital:	Bairiki
Languages:	English
Currency:	Australian dollar

Nacula Island, the Yasawa Islands, Fiji.

Fanning Island, Kiribati.

201

Marshall Islands

The Marshall Islands consist of an archipelago of over 1,000 islands and atolls. Between 1946 and 1958, the U.S.A. tested 64 nuclear weapons on the islands of Bikini and Enewetak, and it is thought that the local population is still suffering from the effects. Once a German protectorate, the Marshall Islands were occupied by the Japanese during the Second World War, but were administered by the U.S.A. as part of the UN Trust Territory of the Pacific from 1947, becoming a republic 'in free association with the U.S.A.' in 1986. The country is still heavily dependent upon U.S. aid.

Population: 56,086
Capital: Majuro
Languages: English
Currency: U.S. dollar

Micronesia

The Federated States of Micronesia cover an archipelago of islands encompassing most of the Caroline Islands in the Pacific Ocean. They constitute a federated state in free association with the U.S.A., having gained their present status in 1985. The flag dates from 1962, the white and light blue being the colors of the UN. The four stars stand for the four states (Kosrai, Pohnpei, Truk and Yap).

Population: 101,351
Capital: Palikir
Languages: English
Currency: U.S. dollar

Nauru

Situated in the middle of the Pacific Ocean, Nauru is a coral atoll lying just south of the equator. It achieved independence in 1968 after having been under a UN trusteeship since 1946. The country is dependent upon the export of phosphate rock, which will eventually become depleted. The flag won a design competition, its 12-pointed star representing the aboriginal people of the island. The star beneath the yellow line (the equator) indicates the location of the country in the Pacific Ocean.

Population: 10,084
Capital: Yaren (de facto)
Languages: English
Currency: Australian dollar

The Ulithi Coral Atoll, Yap State, Micronesia.

New Zealand

Located in the Pacific Ocean, New Zealand is a mountainous country lying on a belt of tectonic activity. It was settled by Maoris in the 8th century, though they may not have been the first inhabitants. The first European to arrive was Abel Tasman in 1642. New Zealand's coasts were

Mount Cook and Lake Pukaki.

Wellington.

charted by James Cook in 1769–1770. It was Britain's aim to take control of the country, claiming the South Island by right of discovery, and the North Island by the Treaty of Weitangi with Maori chiefs in 1840. New Zealand took Dominion status in 1907, with full independence in 1931. The flag dates from 1869. It features the British blue ensign and has a stylized version of the Southern Cross constellation, displaying four of the five stars.

Population:	4,578,430
Capital:	Wellington
Languages:	English, Maori
Currency:	New Zealand dollar

Auckland, New Zealand.

Palau (Belau)

Palau comprises 26 islands and 300 islets, these being mainly mountainous reefs. The islands became independent in 1994, having formerly been part of the UN Trust Territory of the Pacific Islands and were under U.S. administration. The flag bears an off-center yellow disc depicting the moon, which represents national unity and destiny. The blue background stands for the achievement of independence.

Population:	20,901
Capital:	Melekeok
Languages:	English, Palauan
Currency:	U.S. dollar

Traditional huts, Wamena, Papua New Guinea.

Papua New Guinea

Papua New Guinea forms part of Melanesia and occupies the eastern part of the island of New Guinea and a large number of adjacent islands. European contact dates back to the 16th century, although it was not until the 19th century that British and German settlers arrived. Papua New Guinea was ruled by Australia from after the Second World until 1975, after which it became fully independent. The flag, however, dates from 1971, the use of the five stars of the Southern Cross constellation being due to Australian influence. The bird of paradise emblem goes back to the days of German rule and appeared on two previous flags.

Population:	7,398,500
Capital:	Port Moresby
Languages:	English
Currency:	Kina

Islands of Palau.

The Raja Ampat archipelago, Papua New Guinea.

over by New Zealand in 1920 and finally achieved independence in 1962. The flag shows the Southern Cross constellation, a symbol linking Samoa with other countries in the southern hemisphere. The flag dates from 1948, prior to independence.

Samoa

Samoa consists of two large islands, with a number of other islands and islets situated in the Pacific Ocean. The islands were passed to Germany in 1899, although they were taken

Population:	194,320
Capital:	Apia
Languages:	Samoan, English
Currency:	Tala

Solomon Islands

The Solomon Islands lie in the Pacific Ocean, south-east of Papua New Guinea, and were British from 1893 until 1978, when they gained independence and the new flag was adopted. The five-pointed stars, on a background of blue, represent the country's five main islands, surrounded by the Pacific Ocean, with green for the forests and yellow for the sun. The flag was the winning entry in a design competition.

Population:	581,344
Capital:	Honiara
Languages:	English
Currency:	Solomon Islands dollar

Upolu Island, Samoa.

Coastal view of Kukundu, Solomon Islands.

cross has now become Tonga's national emblem.

Population: 103,252
Capital: Nuku'alofa
Languages: Tongan, English
Currency: Pa'anga

Tonga

Situated in the southern Pacific Ocean, Tonga is an archipelago of at least 170 islands. Once a British protectorate, the islands became fully independent in 1970. The flag, dating back to 1875 and still in use, is based on the British red ensign, intended to represent the Christian faith of the nation. The red

Coral dolman, Tonga.

Vanuatu

Vanuatu consists of a group of over 80 islands and islets in the Pacific Ocean. The islands were discovered in 1606 by Captain Cook, who named them the New Hebrides. From 1906, these islands were jointly administered by Britain and France but gained independence in 1980. On the flag, the Y represents the layout of the islands within the sea. Within the angle of the Y is a boar's tusk and fern leaves representing war and peace. The colors of the flag are those of the political party which dominated events at the time of independence.

Population: 264,652
Capital: Port Vila
Languages: Bislama, English, French
Currency: Vanuatu vatu

Tuvalu

Tuvalu means 'eight islands', although there are in fact nine main islands making up the country. Lying in the southern Pacific Ocean, and having been settled by Polynesians since the 14th century, it was claimed by Britain in 1892. The islands became independent in 1978 when the flag was adopted. It is based on the blue ensign, but the background is a much paler blue. The nine golden stars represent the state's main islands.

Population: 11,323
Capital: Fongafale
Languages: English, Tuvaluan
Currency: Australian dollar

A tropical island in Vanuatu.

CHAPTER SEVEN

POPULATED DEPENDENCIES & TERRITORIES

Abu Dhabi

Abu Dhabi is one of the seven sheikhdoms belonging to the United Arab Emirates. It is an oil-rich country, and a source of great wealth for its population. In 1952, these sheikhdoms came together as the Trucial States and were a British protectorate until 1971. There is one flag for the U.A.E., although each emirate has its own, except Sharjah. All the U.A.E. flags are red and white, that of Abu Dhabi being plain red with a white canton in the upper hoist.

Population:	2,330,000
Capital:	Abu Dhabi
Languages:	Arabic
Currency:	U.A.E. dirham

Abu Dhabi.

Ajman

Ajman belongs to the United Arab Emirates and is the smallest, poorest member. Ajman has no oil and little industry and is largely supported by the other member states. The red and white flag is a feature of all the U.A.E. states.

Population:	238,000
Capital:	Ajman
Languages:	Arabic
Currency:	U.A.E. dirham

Sheikh Khalifa Mosque, Ajman.

colonial administration by a British-appointed governor. The flag has the British blue ensign and a shield, within which are three dolphins representing strength, unity and endurance; the white is for peace and the blue for the sea.

American Samoa

Located in the South Pacific Ocean, American Samoa is composed of a group of volcanic islands and atolls, with Tutuila being the largest of the group. Once divided between Germany and Britain, the islands were acquired by the United States in 1899, although the flag was not adopted until 1960. This displays the American eagle grasping a Samoan war club and tribal chief's staff, both symbols of the chief's authority.

Population:	55,519
Capital:	Pago Pago
Languages:	English, Samoan
Currency:	U.S. dollar

Anguilla

Anguilla is a long, thin atoll that is part of the Lesser Antilles or Leeward Islands. Together with the Virgin Islands, it is governed under one

Population:	13,452
Capital:	The Valley
Languages:	English
Currency:	East Caribbean dollar

Anguilla.

Aruba

Aruba is a dry limestone island in the Lesser Antilles. It is a Dutch overseas territory, although it achieved separate status from the other Dutch islands in the area in 1986 and complete internal control. The flag dates from 1976 and shows a four-pointed star representing the island's four main languages.

Population: 107,394
Capital: Oranjestad
Languages: Dutch, Papamiento
Currency: Aruba florin
(= Netherlands
Antilles guilder)

An example of Caribbean architecture, Oranjestad, Aruba.

The Azores have been a dependency of Portugal since 1430, although they were granted a greater degree of autonomy in 1976. The flag dates from 1979 and shows a hawk (or acor), after which the islands were named. The nine stars above the hawk represent the nine islands.

Azores

Situated in the North Atlantic Ocean, the Azores are an amalgamation of nine islands which are part of the mid-Atlantic ridge and volcanic in origin.

Population:	245,746
Capital:	Ponta Delgada
Languages:	Portuguese
Currency:	Euro

Bermuda

First discovered by the Spanish explorer Juan Bermudez, after whom the islands were named, Bermuda is Britain's oldest dependency and has remained so since 1609. Although the blue ensign is the typical flag of the British colonies, Bermuda flies the red ensign, with the shield of its coat of arms on the fly. The coat of arms shows a red lion holding another shield in which the shipwreck of the *Sea Venture* in 1609 is shown.

Population:	64,237
Capital:	Hamilton
Languages:	English
Currency:	Bermuda dollar (= U.S. dollar)

Horta, on Faial Island, Azores.

King's Wharf, Bermuda.

Caribbean Netherlands

The Caribbean Netherlands are three special municipalities of the Netherlands, located in the Caribbean Sea. They consist of the islands of Bonaire, Sint Eustatius and Saba. The islands are currently classified as overseas countries and territories of the European Union.

Population:	23,296
Capitals:	Kralendijk, Oranjestad, The Bottom
Languages:	Dutch
Currency:	Netherlands Antillean guilder

Kralendijk, Bonaire, Caribbean Netherlands.

A village on Saba, Caribbean Netherlands.

Cayman Islands

Situated north-west of Jamaica, the Cayman Islands consist of three low-lying islands. They are a dependent territory of Britain, famous for offshore finance, with tourism also playing an important part in the economy. The Cayman Islands fly the blue ensign, the coat of arms showing an English heraldic lion. The blue wavy lines symbolize the sea.

Population:	55,691
Capital:	Georgetown
Languages:	English
Currency:	Cayman Islands dollar

Christmas Island
(Australia)

The flag of Christmas Island was unofficially adopted in 1986 after it was declared the winner in a competition for a flag for the territory. It was designed by Tony Couch of Sydney, Australia, and was made official on Australia Day in 2002, when the administrator of the territory, Bill Taylor, presented the flag. The flag consists of a green and blue background, dissected from the top left corner to the bottom right. The colors are intended to represent the land and sea respectively, with the stars representing the Southern Cross constellation. There is also a golden bosun bird, which is regarded as a symbol of the island, the central motif being the island itself.

Population:	2,072
Capital:	Flying Fish Cove
Languages:	English
Currency:	Australian dollar

Georgetown, Cayman Islands.

Cocos (Keeling) Islands
(Australia)

The territory of the Cocos (Keeling) Islands, belonging to Australia, is located in the Indian Ocean, south-west of Christmas Island and approximately midway between Australia and Sri Lanka. The territory consists of two atolls and 27 coral islands, of which two, West Island and Home Island, are inhabited. The flag was created in 2003 and adopted in 2004. It is predominantly green, with a palm tree on a golden disc in the canton, a gold crescent in the centre of the flag and a gold Southern Cross constellation on the fly, as in the Australian flag.

Population:	550
Capital:	West Island
Languages:	English
Currency:	Australian dollar

Direction Island, Cocos (Keeling) Islands.

221

Cook Islands

Named after Captain James Cook, the islands were a British protectorate from 1888 until 1901, when they became a dependency of New Zealand. The flag was adopted in 1979 and displays a blue ensign, the 15 stars representing the 15 islands which make up the group.

Population:	14,974
Capital:	Avarua
Languages:	English
Currency:	Cook Islands dollar (= New Zealand dollar)

Dubai

Dubai is the second largest of the United Arab Emirates, the country having formerly been one of the Trucial States before becoming part of the U.A.E. in 1971. Dubai is highly developed and modernized due to the country's great oil wealth. The red and white flag bears the typical colours of the U.A.E. countries.

Population:	2,105,177
Capital:	Dubai
Languages:	Arabic
Currency:	U.A.E. dirham

Aitutaki Lagoon, Cook Islands.

Dubai Marina.

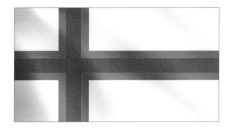

Faeroe Islands

The Faeroe islands are situated in the North Atlantic, south-east of Iceland, the main industries being sheep-farming and fishing. The islands are a dependency of Denmark and have been so since 1386, although they became self-governing in 1948. The flag, featuring the off-center cross, is taken from the Danish flag. Red and blue are both traditional colors of the islands, the white representing the foam of the sea.

Population:	48,724
Capital:	Tórshavn
Languages:	Danish
Currency:	Faroese króna

Faeroe Islands.

King penguins, Falkland Islands.

Falkland Islands

The Falklands consist of two main islands lying off the coast of South America. The country was discovered in 1592 by John Davis. First populated by the French, then by the British, the islands were taken over by Argentina, but have been British since 1833. The Argentinians (who claim the islands and call them Las Malvinas) invaded the Falklands in 1982, but were defeated by the British. The flag displays the blue ensign. The coat of arms within the disc shows John Davis' ship *Desire*, which discovered the islands. The sheep represent the islands' main farming activity.

Population:	3,000
Capital:	Stanley
Languages:	English
Currency:	Falkland Islands Pound (= Pound sterling)

French Guiana

French Guiana is the smallest country on the mainland of South America. It has been a French dependency since 1676 and is treated as part of mainland France, being an official Overseas Department and Administrative Region. In January 2010 the General Council of the Overseas Department of French Guiana unilaterally adopted a flag, which was composed of three colors, the green representing the forests, yellow the gold and other minerals of the region, and the red star socialism.

Population: 239,648
Capital: Cayenne
Languages: French
Currency: Euro

Dreyfus's Tower in Kourou, French Guiana.

French Polynesia

French Polynesia is a group of 130 islands, scattered halfway between Australia and South America, with Tahiti the largest island in the group. The islands became a French protectorate in 1843, but gained increased internal control in 1984 while remaining an overseas territory. As French Polynesia is an Overseas Territory of France, its official flag is the tricolor, although the local flag features the Polynesian colors of red and white. In the central circle is a twin-hulled canoe against a golden sun, which symbolizes fishing and the riches that come from the sea.

Population:	268,270
Capital:	Papeete
Languages:	Tahitian, French
Currency:	French C.F.P (French Pacific franc)

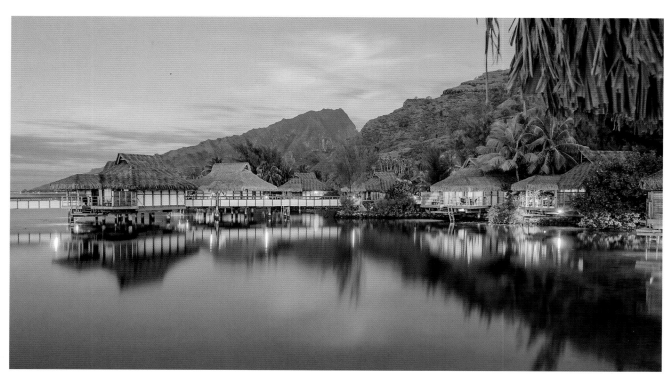

French Polynesia.

Fujairah

Fujairah is one of the smaller of the seven emirates making up the United Arab Emirates. It is one of the poorer regions and it is the only emirate that is without a coastline on the Persian Gulf.

Population:	152,000
Capital:	Fujairah
Languages:	Arabic
Currency:	U.A.E. dirham

Gibraltar

The Rock of Gibraltar lies at the north-eastern end of the Strait of Gibraltar.

Gibraltar was first recognized as a British territory in 1713 and its official flag is the Union Jack. Since 1966, however, the flag showing the castle and key has been used internally, the castle representing Gibraltar's important strategic position on the Mediterranean, as does the key.

Population:	30,001
Capital:	Gibraltar
Languages:	English, Spanish
Currency:	Pound sterling

Rock of Gibraltar.

Greenland

Greenland is a large island in the Arctic with much of the land covered by a huge ice sheet (the world's second largest after Antarctica). The island has been a Danish possession since 1380, although full internal self-government was granted in 1981. The flag was introduced in 1985, as the result of a competition, and reflects the colors of Denmark. It symbolizes the midsummer sun rising over the polar ice.

Population:	55,984
Capital:	Nuuk (Godthab)
Languages:	Danish, Greenlandic
Currency:	Danish krone

Guadeloupe

Guadeloupe encompasses seven Caribbean islands which include Basse-Terre, Grande-Terre, Saint-Martin and Saint-Barthélémy. Guadeloupe is a French Overseas Department and administrative region and therefore has the French tricolor as its flag. In local use, however, is a flag based on the coat of arms of Basse-Terre, which has a red field with a yellow sun and green sugar cane; there is a blue stripe with yellow *fleurs-de-lis* at the top.

Population:	405,739
Capital:	Basse-Terre
Languages:	French
Currency:	Euro

Guam

Guam is the largest of the Mariana group of islands lying in the western Pacific Ocean. The island was colonized by Spain in 1668 but became a dependency of the United States in 1898. The flag dates from 1917 and is flown alongside the 'Stars and Stripes'.

Population:	159,358
Capital:	Hagatna
Languages:	English, Chamorro
Currency:	U.S. dollar

Qeqertarsuaq, Greenland.

Tumon Bay, Guam.

Hong Kong

(China)

Hong Kong comprises Hong Kong Island and the surrounding smaller islands, the Kowloon peninsula and the 'New Territories'. Hong Kong was a British dependency and was acquired in stages. In 1898, Britain received a 99-year lease from the Chinese, which expired in 1997 when Hong Kong reverted to China. The current flag is a stylized, five-petalled Hong Kong orchid tree flower (*Bauhinia blakeana*) in the center of a red field. It was officially hoisted on 1 July 1997 in the handover ceremony marking the transfer of sovereignty.

Population:	7,264,100
Capital:	Hong Kong
Languages:	Chinese, English
Currency:	Hong Kong dollar

Eastern district buildings, Hong Kong.

Hong Kong waterside.

Macao.

Macao
(China)

Macao was a Portuguese colony from 1849, and lies to the west of Hong Kong. In 1979, Macao was redefined as a Chinese territory under Portuguese Administration. The territory was returned to China in 1999.

Population:	636,200
Capital:	Macao
Languages:	Chinese, Portuguese
Currency:	Pataca

Madeira Islands

The Madeira Islands lie off the Moroccan coast in the Atlantic Ocean. The islands are a dependency of Portugal and were first discovered by João Goncalves Zarco in 1419. In 1980 the islands gained partial autonomy. The emblem on the flag dates back to the 15th century, when the islands were first colonized; the cross represents the Order of Christ.

Population:	267,785
Capital:	Funchal
Languages:	Portuguese,
Currency:	Euro

Porto Moniz, Madeira.

233

Colonial houses in Willemstad, Curaçao.

Netherlands Antilles

Composed of five Caribbean islands, in 1954, the dependency gained full self-government. Until 1986, Aruba was the sixth member of the island group when it broke away from Netherlands Antilles and gained complete internal autonomy. The Netherlands Antilles dissolved on 10 October 2010. Curaçoa and Saint Martin became autonomous territories of the Kingdom of the Netherlands. Bonaire, Saba and Saint Eustatius now fall under the direct administration of the Netherlands. (*see also* Dutch Caribbean, page 218).

Population:	304,759
Capital:	Willemstad
Languages:	Dutch, Papamiento, English
Currency:	Netherlands Antillean guilder

New Caledonia

New Caledonia comprises a series of islands in the Pacific Ocean, which have been a French possession since 1853 and an Overseas Territory since 1958. Up until 2010, the only flag used was the French tricolor. In July 2010, however, the Congress of New Caledonia voted in favor of a motion to fly the Kanak flag alongside the French tricolor. The new flag consists of horizontal bands of blue, red and green, the blue representing the sky, the red the sacrifices made in the Kanak's battle for freedom, and the green for the territory and for the predecessors laid to rest. The yellow circle symbolizes the sun and the insignia within it a type of arrow which decorates the tops of Kanak dwellings.

Population:	268,767
Capital:	Nouméa
Languages:	French
Currency:	(CFP) French Pacific Franc

Bourail, New Caledonia.

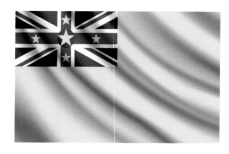

Niue Island

Niue is one of the Polynesian islands which were annexed by New Zealand in 1901; it is a self-governing dependency of New Zealand. The flag shows the Union Jack with the addition of five stars. The yellow background symbolizes the warm relationship between Niue Island and New Zealand.

Population:	1,613
Capital:	Alofi
Languages:	English, Polynesian
Currency:	New Zealand dollar/Niue dollar

Norfolk Island

Halfway between New Caledonia and New Zealand, Norfolk Island was first discovered by Captain Cook in 1774. In 1914, it became a territory of the Australian Commonwealth. The island is known for its pine trees, one of which is represented on its flag. The island is now a Territory of Australia.

Population:	2,392
Capital:	Kingston
Languages:	English
Currency:	Australian dollar

Alofi coastline, Niue.

Northern Mariana Islands

The Northern Mariana Islands lie in the Pacific Ocean and are a Commonwealth Territory of the U.S. They have had internal self-government from 1976. The current flag was adopted in July 1985 by the Second Northern Marianas Constitution, and consists of three symbols, the star for the U.S.A., the *latte* stone for the Chamorros, and the *mwarmwar* for the Carolinians. The shaded blue areas represent the deep waters of the Marianas Trench.

Population:	53,883
Capital:	Saipan
Languages:	English, Chamorro
Currency:	U.S. dollar

Managaha Island and Tanapaq Lagoon, Saipan, Northern Mariana Islands.

Saint Martin

(Collectivity of)

The Collectivity of Saint Martin constitutes the northern half of a Caribbean island which is shared with the Netherlands. The French tricolor is the official flag, although the unofficial flag is also used. This consists of two ribbons representing the sea (blue) and Fort Louis (green), and is said to represent unity.

Population:	35,724
Capital:	Marigot
Languages:	French
Currency:	Euro

Marigot, capital of St. Martin, from Fort St. Louis, St. Martin.

1985, and is a horizontal bicolor of red and blue with the coat of arms of Sint Maarten on a white chevron. The red symbolizes war and bloodshed, the blue peace and assurance of pardon and the white purity and faith.
(*See also* Saint Martin opposite).

Saint Pierre & Miquelon

Saint Pierre and Miquelon is a self-governing territorial overseas collectivity of France, situated in the northwestern Atlantic Ocean near Canada. The flag features a galleon under full sail which depicts the ship that took Jacques Cartier to the territory on 15 June 1536. Blue depicts the Atlantic Ocean and the sky. The three emblems symbolize the first colonists. The Basque country is denoted by a green cross overlaid by a white cross on a red field and Brittany is represented by ermine, and Normandy is represented by two yellow lions.

Population:	6,069
Capital:	Saint-Pierre
Languages:	French
Currency:	Euro

Sint Maarten

Sint Maarten is a country within the Kingdom of the Netherlands occupying the southern half of the island of Saint Martin. The current flag was officially adopted on 13 June

Population:	37,429
Capital:	Philipsburg
Languages:	Dutch
Currency:	Netherlands Antilles guilder

Philipsburg, Sint Maarten.

245

Virgin Islands

The British Virgin Islands are part of the Lesser Antilles group and comprise four main islands. The islands fly the British blue ensign, the badge showing a vestal virgin carrying a lamp. Beneath the shield is a gold scroll with the motto *Vigilate* 'Be Alert'.

The U.S. Virgin islands were first claimed as colonies by Spain, then became Danish and were finally sold to the U.S. in 1917. Dating from 1921, the flag derives from the seal of the U.S.A. The three arrows clutched by the eagle represent the three main islands, with the letters 'V' and 'I' standing for Virgin Islands.

U.S. Virgin Islands

Population:	106,405
Capital:	Charlotte Amalie
Languages:	English
Currency:	U.S. dollar

British Virgin Islands

Population:	28,054
Capital:	Road Town
Languages:	English
Currency:	U.S. dollar

View of Road Town, British Virgin Islands.

248

Charlotte Amalie, St. Thomas, U.S. Virgin Islands.

The flags of the world, flying in First Avenue near the United Nations Building in New York City.

INTERNATIONAL ORGANIZATIONS

Arab League

NATO

Organization of African
Union

Commonwealth

Olympic Games

Red Crescent

European Union

Organization of American
States

International Red Cross

South-East Asia
Organization Treaty

United Nations

INDEX